Measure What Matters

'*Measure What Matters* deserves to be fully embraced by every person responsible for performance, in any walk of life. John Doerr makes Andy Grove a mentor to us all. If every team, leader and individual applied OKRs with rigour and imagination, all sectors of society could see an exponential increase in productivity and innovation'
—Jim Collins, author of *Good to Great*

'John Doerr has taught a generation of entrepreneurs and philanthropists that execution is everything. *Measure What Matters* shows how any organization or team can aim high, move fast and excel'
—Sheryl Sandberg, Facebook COO and founder of LeanIn.org and OptionB.org

'In this indispensable book, the most important venture capitalist of our era reveals a key to business innovation and success. This crisp and colourful book combines fascinating case studies with insightful personal stories to show how OKRs can add magic to organizations of any size'
—Walter Isaacson, author of *Steve Jobs* and *The Innovators*

'*Measure What Matters* takes you behind the scenes for the creation of Intel's powerful OKR systems – one of Andy Grove's finest legacies'
—Gordon Moore, co-founder and former chairman of Intel

'John Doerr is a Silicon Valley legend. He and Kris Duggan explain how transparently setting objectives and defining key results can align organizations and motivate high performance'
—Jonathan Levin, dean of Stanford Graduate School of Business

'*Measure What Matters* is a gift to every leader or entrepreneur who wants a more transparent, accountable and effective team. It encourages the kind of big, bold bets that can transform an organization'
—John Chambers, executive chairman of Cisco

'John Doerr has been the source of management magic for many of the most iconic companies in Silicon Valley that went on to change the world. *Measure What Matters* is a must-read for anyone motivated to improve their organization'
    —Al Gore, former vice president, chairman of the Climate
        Reality Project

ABOUT THE AUTHOR

John Doerr is the chair of venture capital film Kleiner Perkins, which he joined in 1980. By investing in some of the world's most successful entrepreneurs and companies, including Amazon, Google, Intuit, Netscape and Twitter, he has helped create more than 425,000 jobs.

whatmatters.com

Measure
What
Matters

OKRs – the Simple Idea That Drives 10× Growth

John Doerr

PORTFOLIO
PENGUIN

PORTFOLIO PENGUIN

UK | USA | Canada | Ireland | Australia
India | New Zealand | South Africa

Portfolio Penguin is part of the Penguin Random House group of companies
whose addresses can be found at global.penguinrandomhouse.com.

First published in the United States of America by Portfolio/Penguin, an imprint of
Penguin Random House LLC 2018
First published in Great Britain by Portfolio 2018
006

Printed at Thomson Press India Ltd, New Delhi

A CIP catalogue record for this book is available from the British Library

ISBN: 978–0–241–34848–2

www.greenpenguin.co.uk

MIX
Paper from
responsible sources
FSC   FSC® C018179

Penguin Random House is committed to a
sustainable future for our business, our readers
and our planet. This book is made from Forest
Stewardship Council® certified paper.

For Ann, Mary, and Esther
and the wonder of their unconditional love

CONTENTS

PART TWO: The New World of Work

FOREWORD

Larry Page

Alphabet CEO and Google Cofounder

I wish I had had this book nineteen years ago, when we founded Google. Or even before that, when I was only managing myself! As much as I hate process, good ideas with great execution are how you make magic. And that's where OKRs come in.

John Doerr showed up one day in 1999 and delivered a lecture to us on objectives and key results, and how we should run the company based on his experience at Intel. We knew Intel was run well, and John's talk made a lot of intuitive sense, so we decided we'd give it a try. I think it's worked out pretty well for us.

OKRs are a simple process that helps drive varied organizations forward. We have adapted how we use it over the years. Take it as a blueprint and make it yours, based on what you want to see happen!

For leaders, OKRs give a lot of visibility into an organization. They also provide a productive way to push back. For example, you might ask: "Why can't users load a video on YouTube almost instantly? Isn't that more important than this other goal you're planning to do next quarter?"

I'm glad to join in celebrating the memory of Bill Campbell, which John has done very nicely at the conclusion of the book. Bill was a fantastically warm human being who had the gift of almost always being right—especially about people. He was not afraid to tell anyone about how "full of shit" they were, and somehow they would still like him even after that. I miss Bill's weekly haranguing very much. May everyone have a Bill Campbell in their lives—or even strive to make themselves be a bit more like the Coach!

I don't write a lot of forewords. But I agreed to do this one because John gave Google a tremendous gift all those years ago. OKRs have helped lead us to 10x growth, many times over. They've helped make our crazily bold mission of "organizing

Larry Page and John Doerr, 2014.

the world's information" perhaps even achievable. They've kept me and the rest of the company on time and on track when it mattered the most. And I wanted to make sure people heard that.

PART ONE

OKRs in Action

1

Google, Meet OKRs

If you don't know where you're going,
you might not get there.

—Yogi Berra

On a fall day in 1999, in the heart of Silicon Valley, I arrived at a two-story, L-shaped structure off the 101 freeway. It was young Google's headquarters, and I'd come with a gift.

The company had leased the building two months earlier, outgrowing a space above an ice-cream parlor in downtown Palo Alto. Two months before that, I'd placed my biggest bet in nineteen years as a venture capitalist, an $11.8 million wager for 12 percent of a start-up founded by a pair of Stanford grad school dropouts. I joined Google's board. I was committed, financially and emotionally, to do all I could to help it succeed.

Barely a year after incorporating, Google had planted its flag: to "organize the world's information and make it universally accessible and useful." That might have sounded grandiose, but I had confidence in Larry Page and Sergey Brin. They were self-assured, even brash, but also curious and thoughtful. They listened—and they delivered.

Sergey was exuberant, mercurial, strongly opinionated, and able to leap intellectual chasms in a single bound. A Soviet-born immigrant, he was a canny, creative negotiator and a principled leader. Sergey was restless, always pushing for more; he might drop to the floor in the middle of a meeting for a set of push-ups.

Larry was an engineer's engineer, the son of a computer science pioneer. He was a soft-spoken nonconformist, a rebel with a 10x cause: to make the internet exponentially more relevant. While Sergey crafted the commerce of technology, Larry toiled on the product and imagined the impossible. He was a blue-sky thinker with his feet on the ground.

Earlier that year, when the two of them came to my office to pitch me, their PowerPoint deck had just seventeen slides—and only two with numbers. (They added three cartoons just to flesh out the deck.) Though they'd made a small deal with the *Washington Post*, Google had yet to unlock the value of keyword-targeted ads. As the eighteenth search engine to arrive on the web, the company was way late to the party. Ceding the competition such a long head start was normally fatal, especially in technology.*

But none of that stopped Larry from lecturing me on the poor quality of search in the market, and how much it could be improved, and how much bigger it would be tomorrow. He and Sergey had no doubt they would break through, never mind their lack of a business plan. Their PageRank algorithm was that much better than the competition, even in beta.

I asked them, "How big do you think this could be?" I'd already made my private calculation: If everything broke right,

---

* The rare exceptions are true disruptors. Exhibit B: The iPod, which lagged at least nine other digital audio players into commercial production. Within three years, it gulped more than 70 percent of the market.

Larry Page and Sergey Brin at Google's birthplace, the garage at
232 Santa Margarita, Menlo Park, 1999.

Google might reach a market cap of $1 billion. But I wanted to gauge their dreams.

And Larry responded, "Ten billion dollars."

Just to be sure, I said, "You mean market cap, right?"

And Larry shot back, "No, I don't mean market cap. I mean revenue."

I was floored. Assuming a normal growth rate for a profitable tech firm, $10 billion in revenue would imply a $100 billion market capitalization. That was the province of Microsoft and IBM and Intel. That was a creature rarer than a unicorn. There was no braggadocio to Larry, only calm, considered judgment. I didn't debate him; I was genuinely impressed. He and Sergey were determined to change the world, and I believed they had a shot.

Long before Gmail or Android or Chrome, Google brimmed

with big ideas. The founders were quintessential visionaries, with extreme entrepreneurial energy. What they lacked was management experience.* For Google to have real impact, or even to reach liftoff, they would have to learn to make tough choices and keep their team on track. Given their healthy appetite for risk, they'd need to pull the plug on losers—to fail fast.†

Not least, they would need timely, relevant data. To track their progress. To measure what mattered.

And so: On that balmy day in Mountain View, I came with my present for Google, a sharp-edged tool for world-class execution. I'd first used it in the 1970s as an engineer at Intel, where Andy Grove, the greatest manager of his or any era, ran the best-run company I had ever seen. Since joining Kleiner Perkins, the Menlo Park VC firm, I had proselytized Grove's gospel far and wide, to fifty companies or more.

To be clear, I have the utmost reverence for entrepreneurs. I'm an inveterate techie who worships at the altar of innovation. But I'd also watched too many start-ups struggle with growth and scale and getting the right things done. So I'd come to a philosophy, my mantra:

Ideas are easy. Execution is everything.

In the early 1980s, I took a fourteen-month sabbatical from Kleiner to lead the desktop division at Sun Microsystems. Suddenly I found myself in charge of hundreds of people. I was terrified. But Andy Grove's system was my bastion in a storm, a source of clarity in every meeting I led. It empowered my executive team and rallied the whole operation. Yes, we made our share of mis-

---

* In 2001, at my suggestion, the founders recruited Eric Schmidt, my old colleague at Sun Microsystems, to be their CEO. Eric made the trains run on time and broke the ties. Then I introduced Bill Campbell to coach all three of them.

† I'd personally learned this drill at Intel in the 1970s. Gordon Moore, the legend who preceded Andy Grove as Intel's CEO, would say, "I view this year's failure as next year's opportunity to try it again."

takes. But we also achieved amazing things, including a new RISC microprocessor architecture, which secured Sun's lead in the workstation market. That was my personal proof point for what I was bringing, all these years later, to Google.

The practice that molded me at Intel and saved me at Sun—that still inspires me today—is called OKRs. Short for *Objectives* and *Key Results*. It is a collaborative goal-setting protocol for companies, teams, and individuals. Now, OKRs are not a silver bullet. They cannot substitute for sound judgment, strong leadership, or a creative workplace culture. But if those fundamentals are in place, OKRs can guide you to the mountaintop.

Larry and Sergey—with Marissa Mayer, Susan Wojcicki, Salar Kamangar, and thirty or so others, pretty much the whole company at the time—gathered to hear me out. They stood around the ping-pong table (which doubled as their boardroom table), or sprawled in beanbag chairs, dormitory style. My first PowerPoint slide defined OKRs: "A management methodology that helps to ensure that the company focuses efforts on the same important issues throughout the organization."

An *OBJECTIVE*, I explained, is simply *WHAT* is to be achieved, no more and no less. By definition, objectives are significant, concrete, action oriented, and (ideally) inspirational. When properly designed and deployed, they're a vaccine against fuzzy thinking—and fuzzy execution.

KEY RESULTS benchmark and monitor *HOW* we get to the objective. Effective KRs are specific and time-bound, aggressive yet realistic. Most of all, they are measurable and verifiable. (As prize pupil Marissa Mayer would say, "It's not a key result unless it has a number.") You either meet a key result's requirements or you don't; there is no gray area, no room for doubt. At the end of the designated period, typically a quarter, we declare the key result fulfilled or not. Where an objective can be long-lived, rolled over for a year or longer, key results evolve as the work progresses. Once they are all completed, the objective is necessarily achieved. (And if it isn't, the OKR was poorly designed in the first place.)

My objective that day, I told the band of young Googlers, was to build a planning model for their company, as measured by three key results:

KR #1: I would finish my presentation on time.
KR #2: We'd create a sample set of quarterly Google OKRs.
KR #3: I'd gain management agreement for a three-month OKR trial.

By way of illustration, I sketched two OKR scenarios. The first involved a fictional football team whose general manager cascades a top-level objective down through the franchise org chart. The second was a real-life drama to which I'd had a ringside seat: Operation Crush, the campaign to restore Intel's dominance in the microprocessor market. (We'll delve into both in detail later on.)

I closed by recapping a value proposition that is no less compelling today. OKRs surface your primary goals. They channel efforts and coordination. They link diverse operations, lending purpose and unity to the entire organization.

I stopped talking at the ninety-minute mark, right on time. Now it was up to Google.

—————

In 2009, the Harvard Business School published a paper titled "Goals Gone Wild." It led with a catalog of examples of "destructive goal pursuit": exploding Ford Pinto fuel tanks, wholesale gouging by Sears auto repair centers, Enron's recklessly inflated sales targets, the 1996 Mount Everest disaster that left eight climbers dead. Goals, the authors cautioned, were "a prescription-strength medication that requires careful dosing . . . and close supervision." They even posted a warning label: "Goals may cause systematic problems in organizations due to narrowed focus, unethical behavior, increased risk taking, decreased cooperation, and decreased motivation." The dark side of goal setting could swamp any benefits, or so their argument went.

> ⚠ **WARNING!**
>
> Goals may cause systematic problems in organizations due to narrowed focus, unethical behavior, increased risk taking, decreased cooperation, and decreased motivation.
>
> Use care when applying goals in your organization.

The paper struck a chord and is still widely cited. Its caveat is not without merit. Like any management system, OKRs may be executed well or badly; the aim of this book is to help you use them well. But make no mistake. For anyone striving for high performance in the workplace, goals are very necessary things.

In 1968, the year Intel opened shop, a psychology professor at the University of Maryland cast a theory that surely influenced Andy Grove. First, said Edwin Locke, "hard goals" drive performance more effectively than easy goals. Second, *specific* hard goals "produce a higher level of output" than vaguely worded ones.

In the intervening half century, more than a thousand studies have confirmed Locke's discovery as "one of the most tested, and proven, ideas in the whole of management theory." Among experiments in the field, 90 percent confirm that productivity is enhanced by well-defined, challenging goals.

Year after year, Gallup surveys attest to a "worldwide employee engagement crisis." Less than a third of U.S. workers are "involved in, enthusiastic about and committed to their work and workplace." Of those disengaged millions, more than half would leave their company for a raise of 20 percent or less. In the technology sector, two out of three employees think they could find a better job inside of two months.

In business, alienation isn't an abstract, philosophical problem; it saps the bottom line. More highly engaged work groups generate more profit and less attrition. According to Deloitte, the management and leadership consulting firm, issues of "retention and engagement have risen to No. 2 in the minds of business leaders, second only to the challenge of building global leadership."

But exactly *how* do you build engagement? A two-year Deloitte study found that no single factor has more impact than "clearly defined goals that are written down and shared freely. . . . Goals create alignment, clarity, and job satisfaction."

Goal setting isn't bulletproof: "When people have conflicting priorities or unclear, meaningless, or arbitrarily shifting goals, they become frustrated, cynical, and demotivated." An effective goal management system—an OKR system—links goals to a team's broader mission. It respects targets and deadlines while adapting to circumstances. It promotes feedback and celebrates wins, large and small. Most important, it expands our limits. It moves us to strive for what might seem beyond our reach.

As even the "Goals Gone Wild" crowd conceded, goals "can inspire employees and improve performance." That, in a nutshell, was my message for Larry and Sergey and company.

As I opened the floor for questions, my audience seemed intrigued. I guessed they might give OKRs a try, though I couldn't have foreseen the depth of their resolve. Sergey said, "Well, we need to have *some* organizing principle. We don't have one, and this might as well be it." But the marriage of Google and OKRs was anything but random. It was a great impedance match, a seamless gene transcription into Google's messenger RNA. OKRs were an elastic, data-driven apparatus for a freewheeling, data-worshipping enterprise.* They promised transparency for a team that defaulted to open—open source, open systems, open web. They rewarded "good fails" and daring for two of the boldest thinkers of their time.

Google, meet OKRs: a perfect fit.

While Larry and Sergey had few preconceptions about running a business, they knew that writing goals down would make them real.† They loved the notion of laying out what mattered most to them—on one or two succinct pages—and making it public to everyone at Google. They intuitively grasped how OKRs could keep an organization on course through the gales of competition or the tumult of a hockey-stick growth curve.

Along with Eric Schmidt, who two years later became Google's CEO, Larry and Sergey would be tenacious, insistent, even confrontational in their use of OKRs. As Eric told author Steven Levy, "Google's objective is to be the systematic innovator of scale. Innovator means new stuff. And scale means big, systematic ways of looking at things done in a way that's reproducible." Together, the

---

* As Steven Levy wrote in *In the Plex,* "Doerr had Google at metrics."

† In the very beginning, Google relied on "snippets," three- or four-line status reports on each individual's work.

triumvirate brought a decisive ingredient for OKR success: conviction and buy-in at the top.

———

As an investor, I am long on OKRs. As Google and Intel alumni continue to migrate and spread the good word, hundreds of companies of all types and sizes are committing to structured goal setting. OKRs are Swiss Army knives, suited to any environment. We've seen their broadest adoption in tech, where agility and teamwork are absolute imperatives. (In addition to the firms you will hear from in this book, OKR adherents include AOL, Dropbox, LinkedIn, Oracle, Slack, Spotify, and Twitter.) But the system has also been adopted by household names far beyond Silicon Valley: Anheuser-Busch, BMW, Disney, Exxon, Samsung. In today's economy, change is a fact of life. We cannot cling to what's worked and hope for the best. We need a trusty scythe to carve a path ahead of the curve.

At smaller start-ups, where people absolutely need to be pulling in the same direction, OKRs are a survival tool. In the tech sector, in particular, young companies must grow quickly to get funding before their capital runs dry. Structured goals give backers a yardstick for success: *We're going to build this product, and we've proven the market by talking to twenty-five customers, and here's how much they're willing to pay.* At medium-size, rapidly scaling organizations, OKRs are a shared language for execution. They clarify expectations: *What do we need to get done (and fast), and who's working on it?* They keep employees aligned, vertically and horizontally.

In larger enterprises, OKRs are neon-lit road signs. They demolish silos and cultivate connections among far-flung contributors. By enabling frontline autonomy, they give rise to fresh solutions.

And they keep even the most successful organizations stretching for more.

Similar benefits accrue in the not-for-profit world. At the Bill & Melinda Gates Foundation, a $20 billion start-up, OKRs deliver the real-time data that Bill Gates needs to wage war against malaria, polio, and HIV. Sylvia Mathews Burwell, a Gates alumna, ported the process to the federal Office of Management and Budget and later to the Department of Health and Human Services, where it helped the U.S. government fight Ebola.

But perhaps no organization, not even Intel, has scaled OKRs more effectively than Google. While conceptually simple, Andy Grove's regimen demands rigor, commitment, clear thinking, and intentional communication. We're not just making some list and checking it twice. We're building our capacity, our goal muscle, and there is always some pain for meaningful gain. Yet Google's leaders have never faltered. Their hunger for learning and improving remains insatiable.

As Eric Schmidt and Jonathan Rosenberg observed in their book *How Google Works*, OKRs became the "simple tool that institutionalized the founders' 'think big' ethos." In Google's early years, Larry Page set aside two days per quarter to personally scrutinize the OKRs for each and every software engineer. (I'd sit in on some of those reviews, and Larry's analytical legerdemain—his preternatural ability to find coherence in so many moving parts—was unforgettable.) As the company expanded, Larry continued to kick off each quarter with a marathon debate on his leadership team's objectives.

Today, nearly two decades after my slide show at the ping-pong table, OKRs remain a part of Google's daily life. With growth and its attendant complexity, the company's leaders might have settled into more bureaucratic methods or scrapped OKRs for the latest management fad. Instead, they have stayed the course. The system is alive and well. OKRs are the scaffolding for Google's signature home runs, including seven products with a billion or more users apiece: Search, Chrome, Android, Maps, YouTube, Google Play, and Gmail. In 2008, a company-wide OKR rallied all hands around the Code Yellow battle against latency—Google's bête noire, the lag in retrieving data from the cloud. Bottom-up OKRs work hand in glove with "20 percent time," which frees grassroots engineers to dive into promising side projects.

Many companies have a "rule of seven," limiting managers to a maximum of seven direct reports. In some cases, Google has flipped the rule to a *minimum* of seven. (When Jonathan Rosenberg headed Google's product team, he had as many as twenty.) The higher the ratio of reports, the flatter the org chart—which means less top-down oversight, greater frontline autonomy, and more fertile soil for the next breakthrough. OKRs help make all of these good things possible.

In October 2018, for the seventy-fifth consecutive quarter, Google's CEO will lead the entire company to evaluate its progress against top-level objectives and key results. In November and December, each team and product area will develop its own plans for the coming year and distill them into OKRs. The following January, as CEO Sundar Pichai told me, "We'll go back in front of the company and articulate, 'This is our high-level strategy, and here are the OKRs we have written for the year.'"* (In accordance with company tradition, the executive team will also grade

---

* Google originally used quarterly OKRs, then added annual OKRs for a two-track process. Since succeeding Larry Page as CEO, Sundar Pichai has shifted to a one-track, annual framework. To keep the process vital and time-bound goals on track, each department reports its progress quarterly or sometimes every six weeks—de facto key results. Now CEO of Alphabet, Larry sees to it that OKRs are used at the parent company's other subsidiaries. And he still writes his own individual OKRs each quarter.

Google's OKRs from the prior year, with failures unblinkingly dissected.)

Over the following weeks and months, thousands of Googlers will formulate, discuss, revise, and grade their team and individual OKRs. As always, they'll have carte blanche to browse their intranet and see how other teams are measuring success. They'll be able to trace how their work connects up, down, and sideways— how it fits into Google's big picture.

Not quite twenty years later, Larry's jaw-dropping projection now looks conservative. As we go to press, parent company Alphabet's market cap exceeds $700 billion, making it the second-most valuable company in the world. In 2017, for the sixth year in a row, Google ranked number one on *Fortune* magazine's list of "Best Companies to Work For." This runaway success is rooted in strong and stable leadership, a wealth of technical resources, and a values-based culture of transparency, teamwork, and relentless innovation. But OKRs have also played a vital role. I cannot imagine the Googleplex running without them, and neither can Larry or Sergey.

As you will see in the pages to come, objectives and key results drive clarity, accountability, and the uninhibited pursuit of greatness. Take it from Eric Schmidt, who credits OKRs with "changing the course of the company forever."

———

For decades I've been the Johnny Appleseed of OKRs, doing my best to disseminate Andy Grove's genius with my twenty slides and earnest proposition. But I always felt I was skating on the surface, not really getting the job done. A few years ago, I decided it would be worth trying again—in print this time, and in enough depth to do the subject justice. This book—with its companion website, whatmatters.com—is my chance to bring a long-held passion to you, my reader. I hope you find it useful. I can tell you it has changed my life.

I've introduced the OKR system to the world's most ambitious nonprofit and to an iconic Irish rock star. (And you'll hear from them directly.) I've witnessed countless individuals use objectives and key results to grow more disciplined in their thinking, clearer in communication, more purposeful in action. If this book were an OKR, I'd call its objective aspirational: to make people's lives, *your* life, more fulfilling.

Grove was ahead of his time. Acute focus, open sharing, exacting measurement, a license to shoot for the moon—these are the hallmarks of modern goal science. Where OKRs take root, merit trumps seniority. Managers become coaches, mentors, and architects. Actions—and data—speak louder than words.

In sum, objectives and key results are a potent, proven force for operating excellence—for Google, so why not for you?

———

Like OKRs themselves, this book comes in two complementary sections. Part One considers the system's cardinal features and how it turns good ideas into superior execution and workplace satisfaction. We begin with OKRs' origin story at Andy Grove's Intel, where I became a zealous convert. Then come the four OKR "superpowers": focus, align, track, and stretch.

Superpower #1—Focus and Commit to Priorities
(chapters 4, 5, and 6):
High-performance organizations home in on work that's important, and are equally clear on what *doesn't* matter. OKRs impel leaders to make hard choices. They're a precision communication tool for departments, teams, and indi-

vidual contributors. By dispelling confusion, OKRs give us the focus needed to win.

Superpower #2—Align and Connect for Teamwork
(chapters 7, 8, and 9):
With OKR transparency, everyone's goals—from the CEO down—are openly shared. Individuals link their objectives to the company's game plan, identify cross-dependencies, and coordinate with other teams. By connecting each contributor to the organization's success, top-down alignment brings meaning to work. By deepening people's sense of ownership, bottom-up OKRs foster engagement and innovation.

Superpower #3—Track for Accountability *(chapters 10 and 11):*
OKRs are driven by data. They are animated by periodic check-ins, objective grading, and continuous reassessment—all in a spirit of no-judgment accountability. An endangered key result triggers action to get it back on track, or to revise or replace it if warranted.

Superpower #4—Stretch for Amazing *(chapters 12, 13, and 14):*
OKRs motivate us to excel by doing more than we'd thought possible. By testing our limits and affording the freedom to fail, they release our most creative, ambitious selves.

Part Two covers OKRs' applications and implications for the new world of work:

CFRs *(chapters 15 and 16):* The failings of annual performance reviews have sparked a robust alternative—continuous performance management. I will introduce OKRs' younger sibling, CFRs (Conversation, Feedback, Recognition), and show how OKRs and CFRs can team up to lift leaders, contributors, and organizations to a whole new level.

Continuous Improvement (chapter 17): As a case study for structured goal setting and continuous performance management, we see a robotics-powered pizza company deploys OKRs in every aspect of its operations, from the kitchen to marketing and sales.

The Importance of Culture (chapters 18, 19, and 20): Here we'll explore the impact of OKRs on the workplace, and how they ease and expedite culture change.

Along our journey, we'll rove behind the scenes to observe OKRs and CFRs in a dozen very different organizations, from Bono's ONE Campaign in Africa to YouTube and its quest for 10x growth. Collectively these stories demonstrate the range and potential of structured goal setting and continuous performance management, and how they are transforming the way we work.

2

The Father of OKRs

There are so many people working
so hard and achieving so little.

—*Andy Grove*

This all began with an ex-girlfriend I was trying to win back. Ann had dumped me and was working in Silicon Valley, but I didn't know where. It was the summer of 1975, between terms at Harvard Business School. I drove through Yosemite and arrived in the Valley with no job and no place to live. Though my future was unsettled, I could program computers.* While earning my master's in electrical engineering at Rice University, I'd co-founded a company to write graphics software for Burroughs, one of the "Seven Dwarfs" battling IBM for market share. I loved every minute of it.

I'd hoped to land an internship at one of the Valley's venture capital firms, but they all turned me down. One suggested I try a chip company they'd funded in Santa Clara, a place called Intel. I cold-called the highest-ranking Intel person I could get on the phone, Bill Davidow, who headed the microcomputer division. When Bill heard

---

* I had learned on the PDP-11, the enthusiast's minicomputer of choice.

19

I could write benchmarks, he invited me to come down and meet him.

The Santa Clara headquarters was an open expanse of low-walled cubicles, not yet a design cliché. After a brief chat, Bill referred me to his marketing manager, Jim Lally, who referred me on down the line. By five o'clock I'd scored a summer internship at the rising paragon of tech firms. As luck would have it, I found my ex-girlfriend there, too, working just down the corridor. She was not amused when I showed up. (But by Labor Day, Ann and I would be back together.)

Midway through orientation, Bill took me aside and said, "John, let's be clear about something. There's one guy running operations here, and that's Andy Grove." Grove's title was executive vice president; he would wait twelve more years to succeed Gordon Moore as CEO. But Andy was Intel's communicator, its operator par excellence, its taskmaster-in-chief. Everybody knew he was in charge.

By pedigree, Grove was the least likely member of the Intel Trinity that ran the company for three decades. Gordon Moore was the shy and revered deep thinker, author of the eponymous law that underpins the exponential scaling of technology: Computer processing power doubles every two years. Robert Noyce, co-inventor of the integrated circuit (aka the microchip), was the charismatic Mr. Outside, the industry's ambassador, equally at home at a congressional hearing or buying a round of drinks at the Wagon Wheel. (The semiconductor crowd was a hard-partying crowd.)

And then there was András István Gróf, a Hungarian refugee who'd narrowly escaped the Nazis and reached the U.S. at age twenty with no money, little English, and severe hearing loss. He was a coiled and compact man with curly hair and a maniacal drive. By dint of sheer will and brainpower, he rose to the top of

the most admired organization in Silicon Valley and led it to phe-
nomenal success. During Grove's eleven-year tenure as CEO, Intel
would return more than 40 percent per annum to its shareholders, on a par with the arc of Moore's law.

Intel was Grove's laboratory for management innovation. He
loved to teach, and the company reaped the benefits.* A few days

Andy Grove, 1983.

* As did Stanford University, where he gave one hundred hours of his life each year to sixty
graduate business students.

after getting hired, I received a coveted invitation to Intel's Organization, Philosophy, and Economics course, known as iOPEC, a seminar on Intel strategy and operations. Resident professor: Dr. Andy Grove.

In the space of an hour, Grove traced the company's history, year by year. He summarized Intel's core pursuits: a profit margin twice the industry norm, market leadership in any product line it entered, the creation of "challenging jobs" and "growth opportunities" for employees.* Fair enough, I thought, though I'd heard similar things at business school.

Then he said something that left a lasting impression on me. He referenced his previous company, Fairchild, where he'd first met Noyce and Moore and went on to blaze a trail in silicon wafer research. Fairchild was the industry's gold standard, but it had one great flaw: a lack of "achievement orientation."

"Expertise was very much valued there," Andy explained. "That is why people got hired. That's why people got promoted. Their effectiveness at translating that knowledge into actual results was kind of shrugged off." At Intel, he went on, "we tend to be exactly the opposite. It almost doesn't matter what you know. It's what you can do with whatever you know or can acquire and actually accomplish [that] tends to be valued here." Hence the company's slogan: "Intel delivers."

It almost doesn't matter what you know. . . . To claim that knowledge was secondary and execution all-important—well, I wouldn't learn *that* at Harvard. I found the proposition thrilling, a real-world affirmation of accomplishment over credentials. But Grove wasn't finished, and he had saved the best for last. Over a few closing minutes, he outlined a system he'd begun to install in

---

* A video of Grove's seminar can be found at www.whatmatters.com/grove.

1971, when Intel was three years old. It was my first exposure to the art of formal goal setting. I was mesmerized.

A few unvarnished excerpts, straight from the father of OKRs:*

Now, the two key phrases . . . are objectives and the key result. And they match the two purposes. The objective is the direction: "We want to dominate the mid-range microcomputer component business." That's an objective. That's where we're going to go. Key results for this quarter: "Win ten new designs for the 8085" is one key result. It's a milestone. The two are not the same. . . .

The key result has to be measurable. But at the end you can look, and without any arguments: Did I do that or did I not do it? Yes? No? Simple. No judgments in it.

Now, did we dominate the mid-range microcomputer business? That's for us to argue in the years to come, but over the next quarter we'll know whether we've won ten new designs or not.

It was a "very, very simple system," Grove said, knowing simplicity was catnip to an audience of engineers. On its face, the conception seemed logical, commonsensical—and inspiring. Against the stale management orthodoxy of the period, Grove had created something fresh and original. Strictly speaking, however, his "objectives and key results" did not spring from the void. The process had a precursor. In finding his way, Grove had followed the trail of a legendary, Vienna-born gadfly, the first great "modern" business management thinker: Peter Drucker.

---

* Imagine a mild Hungarian accent, which Grove never quite lost.

Our MBO Ancestors

The early-twentieth-century forefathers of management theory, notably Frederick Winslow Taylor and Henry Ford, were the first to measure output systematically and analyze how to get more of it. They held that the most efficient and profitable organization was authoritarian.* Scientific management, Taylor wrote, consists of "knowing exactly what you want men to do and then see that they do it in the best and cheapest way." The results, as Grove noted, were "crisp and hierarchical: there were those who gave orders and those who took orders and executed them without question."

Half a century later, Peter Drucker—professor, journalist, historian—took a wrecking ball to the Taylor-Ford model. He conceived a new management ideal, results-driven yet humanistic. A corporation, he wrote, should be a community "built on trust and respect for the workers—not just a profit machine." Further, he urged that subordinates be consulted on company goals. Instead of traditional crisis management, he proposed a balance of long- and short-range planning, informed by data and enriched by regular conversations among colleagues.

Drucker aimed to map out "a principle of management that will give full scope to individual strength and responsibility and at the same time give common direction of vision and effort, establish team work and harmonize the goals of the individual with

---

* A more progressive model, mostly ignored at the time, was advanced by a Massachusetts social worker named Mary Parker Follett. In her essay "The Giving of Orders" (1926), Follett proposed that power sharing and collaborative decision making between managers and employees led to better business solutions. Where Taylor and Ford saw hierarchy, Follett saw networks.

the common weal." He discerned a basic truth of human nature: When people help choose a course of action, they are more likely to see it through. In 1954, in his landmark book *The Practice of Management*, Drucker codified this principle as "management by objectives and self-control." It became Andy Grove's foundation and the genesis of what we now call the OKR.

By the 1960s, management by objectives—or MBOs, as the process was known—had been adopted by a number of forward-thinking companies. The most prominent was Hewlett-Packard, where it was a part of the celebrated "H-P Way." As these businesses trained their attention on a handful of top priorities, the results were impressive. In a meta-analysis of seventy studies, high commitment to MBOs led to productivity gains of 56 percent, versus 6 percent where commitment was low.

Eventually, though, the limitations of MBOs caught up with them. At many companies, goals were centrally planned and sluggishly trickled down the hierarchy. At others, they became stagnant for lack of frequent updating; or trapped and obscured in silos; or reduced to key performance indicators (KPIs), numbers without soul or context. Most deadly of all, MBOs were commonly tied to salaries and bonuses. If risk taking might be penalized, why chance it? By the 1990s, the system was falling from vogue. Even Drucker soured on it. MBOs, he said, were "just another tool" and "not the great cure for management inefficiency."

Measuring Output

Andy Grove's quantum leap was to apply manufacturing production principles to the "soft professions," the administrative, professional, and managerial ranks. He sought to "create an environment that values and emphasizes output" and to avoid what Drucker termed the "activity trap": "[S]tressing output is the key to increasing productivity, while looking to increase activity can result in just the opposite." On an assembly line, it's easy enough to distinguish output from activity. It gets trickier when employees are paid to think. Grove wrestled with two riddles: How can we define and measure output by knowledge workers? And what can be done to increase it?

Grove was a scientific manager. He read everything in the budding fields of behavioral science and cognitive psychology. While the latest theories offered "a nicer way to get people to work" than in Henry Ford's heyday, controlled university experiments "simply would not show that one style of leadership was better than another. It was hard to escape the conclusion that no optimal management style existed." At Intel, Andy recruited "aggressive introverts" in his own image, people who solved problems quickly, objectively, systematically, and permanently. Following his lead, they were skilled at confronting a problem without attacking the person. They set politics aside to make faster, sounder, more collective decisions.

Intel relied on systems in every facet of its operations. Marking his debt to Drucker, Grove named his goal-setting system "iMBOs," for Intel Management by Objectives. In practice, however, it was very different from the classical MBO. Grove rarely mentioned objectives without tying them to "key results," a term he seems to have coined himself. To avoid confusion, I'll refer to his approach as "OKRs," the acronym I assembled from the master's lexicon. In nearly every respect, the new method negated the old:

MBOs vs. OKRs

MBOs	Intel OKRs
"What"	"What" and "How"
Annual	Quarterly or Monthly
Private and Siloed	Public and Transparent
Top-down	Bottom-up or Sideways (~50%)
Tied to Compensation	Mostly Divorced from Compensation
Risk Averse	Aggressive and Aspirational

By 1975, when I arrived at Intel, Grove's OKR system was in full swing. Every knowledge worker in the company formulated monthly individual objectives and key results. Within days of the iOPEC seminar, my supervisor directed me to do the same. I'd been put to work writing benchmarks for the 8080, Intel's latest entry in the 8-bit microprocessor marketplace, where it reigned supreme. My goal was to show how our chip was faster and generally beat the competition.

My Intel OKRs are mostly lost to the pre-cloud sands of time, but I'll never forget the gist of my first one:

OBJECTIVE

Demonstrate the 8080s superior performance as compared to the Motorola 6800.

KEY RESULTS
(AS MEASURED BY . . .)

1. **Deliver five benchmarks.**
2. **Develop a demo.**
3. **Develop sales training materials for the field force.**
4. **Cell on three customers to prove the material works.**

Intel's Lifeblood

I remember typing out that OKR on an IBM Selectric. (The first commercial laser printer was a year away.) Then I posted a hard copy on my carrel for people to scan as they walked by. I'd never worked at a place where you wrote down your goals, much less where you could see everybody else's, on up to the CEO. I found it illuminating, a beacon of focus. And it was liberating, too. When people came to me mid-quarter with requests to draft new data sheets, I felt I could say no without fear of repercussion. My OKRs backed me. They spelled out my priorities for all to see.

Through the Andy Grove era, OKRs were Intel's lifeblood. They stood front and center at weekly one-on-ones, biweekly staff meetings, monthly and quarterly divisional reviews. That was how Intel managed tens of thousands of people to etch a million lines of silicon or copper to within a millionth of a meter in accuracy. Fabricating semiconductors is a tough business. Without rigor, nothing works; yields plummet, chips fail. OKRs were constant reminders of what our teams needed to be doing. They told us precisely what we were achieving—or not.

Along with writing my benchmarks, I trained Intel's domestic sales team. Weeks passed. Grove got wind that the most knowledgeable person on the 8080 was a twenty-four-year-old intern. One day he grabbed me and said, "Doerr, come to Europe with me." For a summer kid, it was a heady invitation. I joined Grove and his wife, Eva, on a trip to Paris, London, and Munich. We trained the European sales force, called on three big prospects, and won two accounts. I contributed what I could. We dined at Michelin-starred restaurants, where Grove knew his way around a wine list. He took a liking to me; I felt awed in his presence. He was a man who lived life large.

Back in California, Andy had Bill Davidow write a letter to confirm I'd have a job waiting the following year. That summer was an eye-opening, mind-blowing education, to the point where I almost dropped out of Harvard. I figured I could learn more about business by remaining at Intel. I compromised by returning to Massachusetts and working part time on the company's account with Digital Equipment Corporation, helping to drag them kicking and screaming into the microprocessor era. I finished my last semester, raced back to Santa Clara, and stayed at Intel for the next four years.

Andy Grove, OKR Incarnate

The mid-1970s marked the birth of the personal computer industry, a yeasty time for fresh ideas and upstart entrepreneurs. I was low on the totem pole, a first-year product manager, but Grove and I had a relationship. One spring day I grabbed him and drove up to the first West Coast Computer Faire at the San Francisco Civic Auditorium. We found a former Intel executive demonstrating the Apple II, the state of the art for graphical display. I said, "Andy, we've already got the operating system. We make the microchip. We've got the compilers; we've licensed BASIC. Intel should make a personal computer." But as we hiked down the aisles, past vendors hawking plastic bags of chips and parts, Grove took a long look and said, "Eh, these are hobbyists. We're not going into that business." My big dream was dashed. Intel never did enter the PC market.

Though he wasn't demonstrative, Grove could be a compassionate leader. When he saw a manager failing, he would try to find another role—perhaps at a lower level—where the person might succeed and regain some standing and respect. Andy was a problem solver at heart. As one Intel historian observed, he "seemed to know exactly *what* he wanted and *how* he was going to achieve it."* He was sort of a walking OKR.

Intel was born in the era of the Free Speech Movement at Berkeley and the flower children of Haight-Ashbury. Punctuality was out of fashion among the young, even young engineers, and the company found it challenging to get new hires into work on time. Grove's solution was to post a sign-in sheet at the front desk, to log anyone dragging in after 8:05—we called it Andy's Late List. Grove collected the sheet each morning at 9:00 sharp. (On those mornings when I was tardy, I'd try to beat the system by sitting in the parking lot until five minutes after nine.) Nobody knew of anyone who'd been docked. Even so, the list signified the importance of self-discipline in a business with no margin for error.

Grove was hard on everybody, most of all himself. A proudly self-made man, he could be arrogant. He did not suffer fools, or meandering meetings, or ill-formed proposals. (He kept a set of rubber stamps on his desk, including one engraved BULLSHIT.) The best way to solve a management problem, he believed, was through "creative confrontation"—by facing people "bluntly, directly, and unapologetically."†

Despite Andy's hot temper, he was down-to-earth and approachable, open to any good idea. As he once told *The New York*

---

* Emphasis added.

† We can see Grove's influence on Steve Jobs, with whom he had a very close and very complicated relationship.

Times, Intel managers "leave our stripes outside when we go into a meeting." Every big decision, he believed, should begin with a "free discussion stage . . . an inherently egalitarian process." The way to get his respect was to disagree and stand your ground and, ideally, be shown to be right in the end.

After I'd logged eighteen months as a product manager, Jim Lally—by then the head of systems marketing, and a great mentor and hero of mine—said to me, "Doerr, if you want to be a really good general manager someday, you need to get out in the field, sell, get rejected, and learn to meet a quota. You can have all the technical expertise in the world, but you'll succeed or fail in this business based on whether your team makes their numbers."

I chose Chicago. In 1978, after Ann and I got married, I became a technical sales rep in the Midwest region. It was the best job I've ever had. I loved helping our customers make a better dialysis machine or traffic-light controller. I loved selling Intel microprocessors, the brains of the computer, and I was pretty good at it. (I came by this talent honestly; my father, Lou Doerr, was a mechanical engineer who loved people and loved selling to them.) Since I'd written all the benchmarks, I knew the programming cold. My sales quota that first year was an intimidating $1 million, but I beat it.

After Chicago, I returned to Santa Clara as a marketing manager. Suddenly I had to hire a small team, guide my people's work, and measure it against expectations. My skill set was stretched, and that's when I came to more fully appreciate Grove's goal-setting system. With an Intel manager coaching me through the process, I developed more discipline, more constancy. I relied on OKRs to communicate more clearly and help my team get our most important work done. None of this came naturally. It was a second, deeper level of learning objectives and key results.

In 1980, an opportunity surfaced at Kleiner Perkins to leverage my technical background in working with new companies. Andy could not fathom why I would want to leave Intel. (He himself put the company ahead of everything, with the possible exception of his grandchildren.) He had an amazing ability to reach into your chest and grab your heart, pull it out, and hold it in his hands in front of you. By then he was the company's president, and he said, "Come on, Doerr, don't you want to be a general manager and own a real P&L? I'll let you run Intel's software division." It was a nonexistent business, but could have been built into one. Then he added a zinger: "John, venture capital, that's not a real job. It's like being a real estate agent."

Andy Grove's Legacy

When Grove died at seventy-nine after years of stoic suffering with Parkinson's disease, *The New York Times* called him "one of the most acclaimed and influential personalities of the computer and Internet era." He wasn't an immortal theorist like Gordon Moore or an iconic public figure like Bob Noyce. Nor did he publish enough to rest beside Peter Drucker in the pantheon of management philosophy. Yet Grove changed the way we live. In 1997, three decades after his experiments at Fairchild, he was named *Time* magazine's Man of the Year, "the person most responsible for the amazing growth in the power and the innovative potential of microchips." Andy Grove was a rare hybrid, a supreme technologist and the greatest chief executive of his day. We sorely miss him.

Dr. Grove's Basic OKR Hygiene

The essence of a healthy OKR culture—ruthless intellectual honesty, a disregard for self-interest, deep allegiance to the team—flowed from the fiber of Andy Grove's being. But it was Grove's nuts-and-bolts approach, his engineer's mentality, that made the system work. OKRs are his legacy, his most valuable and lasting management practice. Here are some lessons I learned at Intel from the master and from Jim Lally, Andy's OKR disciple and my mentor:

Less is more. "A few extremely well-chosen objectives," Grove wrote, "impart a clear message about what we say 'yes' to and what we say 'no' to." A limit of three to five OKRs per cycle leads companies, teams, and individuals to choose what matters most. In general, each objective should be tied to five or fewer key results. (See chapter 4, "Superpower #1: Focus and Commit to Priorities.")

Set goals from the bottom up. To promote engagement, teams and individuals should be encouraged to create roughly half of their own OKRs, in consultation with managers. When all goals are set top-down, motivation is corroded. (See chapter 7, "Superpower #2: Align and Connect for Teamwork.")

No dictating. OKRs are a cooperative social contract to establish priorities and define how progress will be measured. Even after company objectives are closed to debate, their key results continue to be negotiated. Collective agreement is essential to maximum goal achievement. (See chapter 7, "Superpower #2: Align and Connect for Teamwork.")

Stay flexible. If the climate has changed and an objective no longer seems practical or relevant as written, key results can be modified or even discarded mid-cycle. (See chapter 10, "Superpower #3: Track for Accountability.")

Dare to fail. "Output will tend to be greater," Grove wrote, "when everybody strives for a level of achievement beyond [their] immediate grasp.... Such goal-setting is extremely important if what you want is peak performance from yourself and your subordinates." While certain operational objectives must be met in full, aspirational OKRs should be uncomfortable and possibly unattainable. "Stretched goals," as Grove called them, push organizations to new heights. (See chapter 12, "Superpower #4: Stretch for Amazing.")

A tool, not a weapon. The OKR system, Grove wrote, "is meant to pace a person—to put a stopwatch in his own hand so he can gauge his own performance. It is not a legal document upon which to base a performance review." To encourage risk taking and prevent sandbagging, OKRs and bonuses are best kept separate. (See chapter 15, "Continuous Performance Management: OKRs and CFRs.")

Be patient; be resolute. Every process requires trial and error. As Grove told his iOPEC students, Intel "stumbled a lot of times" after adopting OKRs: "We didn't fully understand the principal purpose of it. And we are kind of doing better with it as time goes on." An organization may need up to four or five quarterly cycles to fully embrace the system, and even more than that to build mature goal muscle.

3

Operation Crush:
An Intel Story

Bill Davidow
Former Vice President,
Microcomputer Systems Division

Operation Crush—the fight for survival by a young Intel Corporation—is the subject of our first extended story on OKRs. Crush illustrates all four OKR superpowers: focus, alignment, tracking, and stretching. Most of all, it shows how this goal-setting system can move multiple departments and thousands of individuals toward a common objective.

Near the end of my time at Intel, the company faced an existential threat. Led by Andy Grove, top management rebooted the company's priorities in four weeks. OKRs allowed Intel to execute its battle plan with clarity, precision, and lightning speed. The entire workforce shifted gears to focus together on one prodigious goal.

Back in 1971, the Intel engineer Ted Hoff invented the original microprocessor, the multipurpose "computer-on-a-chip." In 1975, Bill Gates and Paul Allen programmed the third-generation Intel 8080 and launched the personal computer revolution. By 1978, Intel had developed the first high-performance, 16-bit microprocessor, the 8086, which found a ready market. But soon it was getting beaten to a pulp by two chips that were faster and easier to program, Motorola's 68000 and upstart Zilog's Z8000.

In late November 1979, a district sales manager named Don Buckout shot off a desperate eight-page telex. Buckout's boss, Casey Powell, sent it on to Andy Grove, then Intel's president and chief operating officer. The communiqué set off a five-alarm fire—and a corporate crusade. Within a week, the executive staff had met to confront the bad news. One week after that, a blue-ribbon task force convened to map out Intel's counteroffensive. Zilog, all agreed, wasn't a serious threat. But Motorola, an industry Goliath and international brand, posed a clear and present danger. Jim Lally set the tone for the war to come:

> There's only one company competing with us, and that's Motorola. The 68000 is the competition. We have to kill Motorola, that's the name of the game. We have to crush the f—king bastards. We're gonna roll over Motorola and make sure they don't come back again.

That became the rallying cry for Operation Crush,* the campaign to restore Intel to its rightful place as market leader. By January 1980, armed with Andy Grove videos to exhort the troops, Crush teams were dispatched to field offices around the globe. By the second quarter, Intel's salespeople had fully deployed the new strategy. By the third quarter, they were on their way toward meeting one of the most daring objectives in the history of tech: two thousand "design wins," the crucial agreements for clients to

---

* The name was inspired by the Denver Broncos' smothering "Orange Crush" defense of the late 1970s.

put the 8086 in their appliances and devices. By the end of that calendar year, they'd routed the enemy and won a resounding victory.

Not one Intel product was modified for Crush. But Grove and his executive team altered the terms of engagement. They revamped their marketing to play to the company's strengths. They steered their customers to see the value of long-term systems and services versus short-term ease of use. They stopped selling to programmers and started selling to CEOs.

Grove "volunteered" Bill Davidow, head of Intel's microcomputer systems division, to lead the operation. Over his long career as an engineer, industry executive, marketing maven, venture investor, thinker, and author, Bill has made many lasting contributions. But one is especially dear to my heart. Bill grafted the critical connective tissue—the phrase "as measured by," or a.m.b.—into Intel's company OKRs. For example, "We will achieve a certain OBJECTIVE *as measured by* the following KEY RESULTS. . . ." Bill's a.m.b made the implicit explicit to all.

At a 2013 panel discussion hosted by the Computer History Museum, Crush veterans recalled the importance of structured goal setting at Intel—and how objectives and key results were used "down into the trenches." The OKRs for Operation Crush, which are sampled on page 42, were classics of the genre: time bound and unambiguous, with every *what* and *how* in place. Best of all, they worked.

As Jim Lally told me: "I was a skeptic on objectives and key results until Grove sat down with me and explained why they mattered. If you tell everybody to go to the center of Europe, and some start marching off to France, and some to Germany, and some to Italy, that's no good—not if you want them all going to Switzerland. If the vectors point in different directions, they add up to zero. But if you get everybody pointing in the same direction, you maximize the results. That was the pitch Grove gave me—and then he told me I had to teach it."

As Bill Davidow recounts here, OKRs were Grove's secret weapon in Operation Crush. They turbocharged a large and multifaceted organization, then propelled it with surprising agility. Up against a unified, goal-driven Intel, Motorola never stood a chance.

———

Bill Davidow: The key result system was Andy Grove's way to mold behavior. Andy had a single-minded commitment to making Intel great. He discouraged people from serving on outside boards; Intel was supposed to be your life. Your objectives and key results consolidated that commitment.

When you're really high up in management, you're teaching—that's what Andy did. Objectives and key results were embedded in the management system at Intel, but they were also a philosophy, a seminal teaching system. We were all taught that if you measured it, things got better.

We wrote our top-level goals with Andy in our executive staff meetings. We sat around the table and decided: "This is it." As a division manager, I adopted any relevant company key results as my objectives. I brought them to my executive team, and we'd spend the next week talking about what we would do that quarter.

What made the system so strong is that Andy would say, "This is what the corporation is going to do," and everybody would go all out to support the effort. We were part of a winning team, and we wanted to keep winning.

At lower levels, people's objectives and key results might encompass close to a hundred percent of their work output. But man-

Andy Grove and Bill Davidow, Intel headquarters, 1980.

agers had additional day-to-day responsibilities. If my objective is to grow a beautiful rose bush, I know without asking that you also want me to keep the lawn green. I doubt I ever had a key result that said, "Walk around to stay on top of employees' morale." We wrote down the things that needed special emphasis.

Intel's Urgency

In December 1979, I went into Andy Grove's executive staff meeting full of complaints. I thought the microprocessor people could do a better job of racking up design wins for the 8086. I wanted to goad them into fighting back and believing in themselves again. And then Andy tagged me and told me to "solve the problem." Operation Crush became my job.

The 8086 didn't bring in so much revenue in and of itself, but it had a broad ripple effect. My division sold design aids—software development systems—for systems using Intel microprocessors. Though we were growing like crazy, we were still dependent on customers' choosing Intel's microchip for their products. Once Intel got its foot in the door with the 8086, we'd get EPROM [the programmable, read-only-memory chip invented at Intel in 1971] and peripheral and controller chip contracts as well. In total, they might be worth ten times the original sale. But if the 8086 went away, my systems business went away, too.

So the stakes were high. After making its reputation as a supplier of memory chips, Intel was under siege. Recently we'd lost the lead on DRAM [the most widely used and economical type of computer memory] to a start-up, and couldn't seem to regain our momentum. Japanese companies were spoiling to invade our beachhead in the lucrative market for EPROM. Microprocessors were Intel's best hope for the future, and we had to get back on top. I can still remember the first slide of one early presentation:

Crush, the purpose: To establish a sense of urgency and set in motion critical, corporate-wide decisions and action plans to address a life-threatening competitive challenge.

Our task force convened on Tuesday, December 4. We met for three days running, many hours a day. It was an intellectual challenge, like solving an enormous puzzle. There was no time to rebuild the 8086, so we spent most of our time figuring out just what we had to sell and how to regain a competitive advantage over Motorola.

I thought we could win by creating a new narrative. We needed to convince our customers that the microprocessor they chose today would be their most important decision for the next decade. Sure, Motorola could come in and say, "We've got a cleaner instruction set." But they couldn't match our broad product family or system-level performance. They couldn't compete with our superb technical support or low cost of ownership. With Intel peripherals, we'd remind people, your products get to market faster and cheaper. With Intel design aids, your engineers work more efficiently.

Motorola was a big, diverse company that made everything from two-way radios to pocket televisions. Intel was a technology leader that stuck to memory chips and microprocessors and systems that supported them. Who would you rather call when something went wrong? Who would you count on to stay in the vanguard?

We had a lot of good ideas that needed to be woven together. Jim Lally wrote them on the whiteboard: "Publish a future products catalog"; "Develop a sales pitch for fifty seminars—and attendees get a catalog." By Friday, we had a plan to mobilize the company. By the following Tuesday, we had approval for a nine-part program—including a multimillion-dollar ad spend, something Intel had never done before. Within a week after that, the strategy went out to the sales force, which was eager to sign on. They'd alerted us to the crisis in the first place, after all.

All that happened before Christmas.

Motorola was extremely well run, but it had a different sense of urgency. When Casey Powell smacked us between the eyes, we responded within two weeks. When we smacked Motorola between the eyes, they couldn't move nearly so fast. A manager there told me, "I couldn't get a plane ticket from Chicago to Arizona approved in the time you took to launch your campaign."

Intel excelled at declaring great generalizations and translating them into actionable, coordinated programs. Each of our nine projects became a company key result. Here's an Intel Crush corporate OKR and a related engineering OKR from the second quarter of 1980:

> ### INTEL CORPORATE OBJECTIVE
> Establish the 8086 as the highest performance 16-bit microprocessor family, as measured by:
>
> ### KEY RESULTS (Q2 1980)
> 1. Develop and publish five benchmarks showing superior 8086 family performance (Applications).
> 2. Repackage the entire 8086 family of products (Marketing).
> 3. Get the 8MHz part into production (Engineering, Manufacturing).
> 4. Sample the arithmetic coprocessor no later than June 15 (Engineering).

> ### ENGINEERING DEPARTMENT OBJECTIVE (Q2 1980)
> Deliver 500 8MHz 8086 parts to CGW by May 30.
>
> ### KEY RESULTS
> 1. Develop final art to photo plot by April 5.
> 2. Deliver Rev 2.3 masks to fab on April 9.
> 3. Test tapes completed by May 15.
> 4. Fab red tag start no later than May 1.

Turning on a Dime

Early on, just after the first of the year, Bob Noyce and Andy Grove staged a Crush kickoff at the San Jose Hyatt House. Their directive to Intel's management corps was simple and clear: "We're going to win in 16-bit microprocessors. We're committed to this." Andy told us what we had to do and why we had to do it, and that we should consider it a priority until it was done.

There were close to one hundred people at the meeting. The message penetrated two levels of management off the bat, and to a third level within twenty-four hours. Word spread awfully fast. Intel was close to a billion-dollar company at the time, and it turned on a dime. To this day, I have never seen anything like it.

And it couldn't have happened without the key result system. If Andy had run the San Jose meeting without it, how could he have simultaneously kicked off all those Crush activities? I can't tell you how many times I've seen people walk out of meetings saying, "I'm going to conquer the world" . . . and three months later, nothing has happened. You get people whipped up with enthusiasm, but they don't know what to do with it. In a crisis, you need a system that can drive transformation—quickly. That's what the key result system did for Intel. It gave management a tool for rapid implementation. And when people reported on what they'd gotten done, we had black-and-white criteria for assessment.

Crush was a thoroughly cascaded set of OKRs, heavily driven from the top, but with input from below. At Andy Grove's level, or even my level, you couldn't know all the mechanics of *how* the battle should be won. A lot of this stuff has to flow uphill. You can tell people to clean up a mess, but should you be telling them which broom to use? When top management was saying "We've got to

INTEL CORPORATION
3065 Bowers Avenue
Santa Clara, California 95051
(408) 987-8080

TO: All Intel Field Sales Engineers

From: Andy Grove

Subject: OPERATION CRUSH

OPERATION CRUSH is the largest and most important marketing offensive we have ever undertaken. It is large in terms of our commitment--it is the corporation's number one key result; it is large in terms of the manpower we have devoted to it--more than 50 man-years of CRUSH effort in the next six months alone; and it is large in terms of its impact on Intel's revenue--over $100 million in revenue over the next three years.

The importance of OPERATION CRUSH does not come from its size and business impact alone though. Strategically the success of this campaign will highlight a significant evolution that has taken place--and will continue to take place--in our business. We intend to establish ourselves as offering complete computer system solutions--in VLSI form. The 4 CPU's, 15 peripheral devices, 25 software products, and 12 system level products we will be announcing over the next 18 months are the most tangible and meaningful testimonials to the reality of this strategy. OPERATION CRUSH represents the articulation of this strategy.

As an Intel Sales Engineer you will play a major role in making OPERATION CRUSH a success. We are counting on your efforts in two major areas:

  • Sell our total microcomputer solution. Use the information in this notebook and follow on material to sell your customers on the need for a complete and integrated microcomputer solution including both hardware and software, rather than just a set of components.

  • Exploit all of Intel's resources to win current designs. Take the lead in formulating action plans that take advantage of all the OPERATION CRUSH resources described in the accompanying material.

With your help, I know OPERATION CRUSH and the Intel of the 1980's will succeed!

Andy Grove marshals the troops for Operation Crush, January 1980.

44

crush Motorola!" somebody at the bottom might have said "Our benchmarks are lousy; I think I'll write some better benchmarks." That was how we worked.

The Greater Good

Intel stayed on a war footing for six months. I was in a staff position, with no line authority, but I got whatever I needed because the whole company knew how much it mattered to Andy. When the key results came back from Intel's divisions, there was virtually no dissent. Everybody was on board. We redirected resources on the fly; I don't think I even had a budget.

Operation Crush ultimately included top management, the entire sales force, four different marketing departments, and three geographic locations—all pulling together as one.* What made Intel different was that it was so apolitical. Managers sacrificed their little fiefdoms for the greater good. Say the microprocessors division was putting out the futures catalog. Somebody might notice, "Oh my God, we've got a peripheral missing"—and that would ripple out to the peripherals division and the allocation of engineering resources. The sales force organized the seminars, but they leaned on application engineers and marketing, and on my division, too. Corporate communications wrangled articles for the trade press from all over the company. It was a total organizational effort.

When I think about Crush, I still can't believe we pulled it off. I guess the lesson is that culture counts. Andy always wanted people to bring problems to management's attention. A field engineer tells his general manager, "You turkeys don't understand what's happen-

---

* Of Intel's two thousand employees at the time, more than half were detailed to Crush. Everybody else was on call.

ing in the market," and within two weeks, the whole company is realigned, top to bottom. Everyone's agreed: "The whistleblower is right. We've got to act differently." It was terribly important that Don Buckout and Casey Powell felt they could speak their minds without retribution. Without that, there's no Operation Crush.

———

Andy Grove was accustomed to having the last word, so let's give it to him here. "Bad companies," Andy wrote, "are destroyed by crisis. Good companies survive them. Great companies are improved by them." So it was for Operation Crush. By 1986, when Intel dumped its formative memory-chip business to go all-in on microprocessors, the 8086 had recaptured 85 percent of the 16-bit market. A bargain-priced variant, the 8088, found fame and fortune inside the first IBM PC, which would standardize the personal computer platform. Today, tens of billions of microcontrollers—in computers and cars, smart thermostats and blood-bank centrifuges—all run on Intel architecture.

And as we've seen, none of this would have happened without OKRs.

4

Superpower #1: Focus and Commit to Priorities

It is our choices . . . that show what we truly
are, far more than our abilities.

—*J. K. Rowling*

Measuring what matters begins with the question: *What is most important for the next three (or six, or twelve) months?* Successful organizations *focus* on the handful of initiatives that can make a real difference, deferring less urgent ones. Their leaders *commit* to those choices in word and deed. By standing firmly behind a few top-line OKRs, they give their teams a compass and a baseline for assessment. (Wrong decisions can be corrected once results begin to roll in. Nondecisions—or hastily abandoned ones—teach us nothing.) *What are our main priorities for the coming period? Where should people concentrate their efforts?* An effective goal-setting system starts with disciplined thinking at the top, with leaders who invest the time and energy to choose what counts.

While paring back a list of goals is invariably a challenge, it is well worth the effort. As any seasoned leader will tell you, no one individual—or company—can "do it all." With a select set of OKRs, we can highlight a few things—the vital things—that must get done, as planned and on time.

In the Beginning . . .

For organization-level OKRs, the buck stops with senior leadership. They must personally commit to the process.

Where do they begin? How do they decide what truly matters most? Google turned to its mission statement: *Organize the world's information and make it universally accessible and useful.* Android, Google Earth, Chrome, the new-and-improved YouTube search engine—these products and dozens more share a common lineage. In each case, the impetus for development came from the founders and executive team, who made plain their focus and commitment through objectives and key results.

But good ideas aren't bound by hierarchy. The most powerful and energizing OKRs often originate with frontline contributors. As a YouTube product manager, Rick Klau was responsible for the site's homepage, the third most visited in the world. The hitch: Only a small fraction of users logged in to the site. They were missing out on important features, from saving videos to channel subscriptions. Much of YouTube's value was effectively hidden to hundreds of millions of people around the world. Meanwhile, the company was forfeiting priceless data. To solve the problem, Rick's team devised a six-month OKR to improve the site's login experience. They made their case to YouTube CEO Salar Kamangar, who consulted with Google CEO Larry Page. Larry opted to elevate the login objective to a Google company-wide OKR, but with a caveat: The deadline would be three months, not six.

When an OKR rises to the top line, "all eyes in the company are on your team," Rick says. "That's a lot of eyes! We had no idea how we'd do it in three months, but we understood that owning a company-level OKR showed that our work took priority." By adding so much emphasis to a product manager's goal, Larry clarified things for other teams, too. As in Operation Crush, everyone rallied to help Rick's group succeed. The YouTube cadre finished on time, though they shipped one week late.

Regardless of how leaders choose a company's top-line goals, they also need goals of their own. Just as values cannot be transmitted by memo,* structured goal setting won't take root by fiat. As you'll see in chapter 6, Nuna's Jini Kim discovered the hard way that OKRs require a public commitment by leadership, in word and deed. When I hear CEOs say "All my goals are team goals," it's a red flag. Talking a good OKR game is not enough. To quote the late, great Bill Campbell, the Intuit CEO who later coached the Google executive team: "When you're the CEO or the founder of a company . . . you've got to say 'This is what we're doing,' and then you have to model it. Because if you don't model it, no one's going to do it."

Communicate with Clarity

For sound decision making, esprit de corps, and superior performance, top-line goals must be clearly understood throughout the organization. Yet by their own admission, two of three companies

---

* As observed by Andy Grove in *High Output Management*.

fail to communicate these goals consistently. In a survey of eleven thousand senior executives and managers, a majority couldn't name their company's top priorities. Only half could name even one.

Leaders must get across the *why* as well as the *what*. Their people need more than milestones for motivation. They are thirsting for meaning, to understand how their goals relate to the mission. And the process can't stop with unveiling top-line OKRs at a quarterly all-hands meeting. As LinkedIn CEO Jeff Weiner likes to say, "When you are tired of saying it, people are starting to hear it."

Key Results: Care and Feeding

Objectives and key results are the yin and yang of goal setting—principle and practice, vision and execution. Objectives are the stuff of inspiration and far horizons. Key results are more earthbound and metric-driven. They typically include hard numbers for one or more gauges: revenue, growth, active users, quality, safety, market share, customer engagement. To make reliable progress, as Peter Drucker noted, a manager "must be able to measure . . . performance and results against the goal."

In other words: Key results are the levers you pull, the marks you hit to achieve the goal. If an objective is well framed, three to five KRs will usually be adequate to reach it. Too many can dilute focus and obscure progress. Besides, each key result should be a challenge in its own right. If you're certain you're going to nail it, you're probably not pushing hard enough.

What, How, When

Since OKRs are a shock to the established order, it may make sense to ease into them. Some companies begin with an annual cycle as they transition from private to public goal setting, or from a top-down process to a more collaborative one. The best practice may be a parallel, dual cadence, with short-horizon OKRs (for the here and now) supporting annual OKRs and longer-term strategies. Keep in mind, though, that it's the shorter-term goals that drive the actual work. They keep annual plans honest—and executed.

Clear-cut time frames intensify our focus and commitment; nothing moves us forward like a deadline. To win in the global marketplace, organizations need to be more nimble than ever before. In my experience, a quarterly OKR cadence is best suited to keep pace with today's fast-changing markets. A three-month horizon curbs procrastination and leads to real performance gains. In *High Output Management*, his leadership bible, Andy Grove notes:

> For the feedback to be effective, it must be received very soon after the activity it is measuring occurs. Accordingly, an [OKR] system should set objectives for a relatively short period. For example, if we plan on a yearly basis, the corresponding [OKR] time should be at least as often as quarterly or perhaps even monthly.

There is no religion to this protocol, no one-size-fits-all. An engineering team might opt for six-week OKR cycles to stay in sync with development sprints. A monthly cycle could do the trick for an early-stage company still finding its product-market fit. The best OKR cadence is the one that fits the context and cul-ture of your business.

Pairing Key Results

The history of the infamous Ford Pinto shows the hazards of one-dimensional OKRs. In 1971, after bleeding market share to more fuel-efficient models from Japan and Germany, Ford countered with the Pinto, a budget-priced subcompact. To meet CEO Lee Iacocca's aggressive demands, product managers skipped over safety checks in planning and development. For example: The new model's gas tank was placed six inches in front of a flimsy rear bumper.

The Pinto was a firetrap, and Ford's engineers knew it. But the company's heavily marketed, metric-driven goals—"under 2,000 pounds and under $2,000"—were enforced by Iacocca "with an iron hand. . . . [W]hen a crash test found that [a] one-pound, one-dollar piece of plastic stopped the puncture of the gas tank, it was thrown out as extra cost and extra weight." The Pinto's in-house green book cited three product objectives: "True Subcompact" (size, weight); "Low Cost of Ownership" (initial price, fuel consumption, reliabil-ity, serviceability); and "Clear Product Superiority" (appearance, comfort, features, ride and handling, performance). Safety was nowhere on the list.

Hundreds of people died after Pintos were rear-ended, and thousands more were severely injured. In 1978, Ford paid the price with a recall of 1.5 million Pintos and sister model Mercury

Bobcats, the largest in automotive history. The company's balance sheet and reputation took a justified beating.

Looking back, Ford didn't lack for objectives or key results. But its goal-setting process was fatally flawed: "The specific, challenging goals were met (speed to market, fuel efficiency, and cost) at the expense of other important features that were not specified (safety, ethical behavior, and company reputation)."

For a more recent cautionary tale, consider Wells Fargo, still reeling from a consumer banking scandal that stemmed from ruthless, one-dimensional sales targets. Branch managers felt pressured to open millions of fraudulent accounts that customers neither wanted nor needed. In one case, a manager's teenage daughter had twenty-four accounts, her husband twenty-one. In the fallout, more than five thousand bankers were fired; the company's credit card and checking account businesses plunged by half or more. The Wells Fargo brand may be damaged beyond repair.

The more ambitious the OKR, the greater the risk of overlooking a vital criterion. To safeguard quality while pushing for quantitative deliverables, one solution is to pair key results—to measure "both effect and counter-effect," as Grove wrote in *High Output Management*. When key results focus on output, Grove noted:

> [T]heir paired counterparts should stress the quality of [the] work. Thus, in accounts payable, the number of vouchers processed should be paired with the number of errors found either by auditing or by our suppliers. For another example, the number of square feet cleaned by a custodial group should be

paired with a . . . rating of the quality of work as assessed by a senior manager with an office in that building.

Table 4.1: Key Results Paired for Quantity and Quality

Quantity Goal	Quality Goal	Result
Three new features	Fewer than five bugs per feature in quality assurance testing	Developers will write cleaner code.
$50M in Q1 sales	$10M in Q1 maintenance contracts	Sustained attention by sales professionals will increase customer success and satisfaction rates.
Ten sales calls	Two new orders	Lead quality will improve to meet the new order threshold requirement.

The Perfect and the Good

Google CEO Sundar Pichai once told me that his team often "agonized" over their goal-setting process: "There are single OKR lines on which you can spend an hour and a half thinking, to make sure we are focused on doing something better for the user." That's part of the territory. But to paraphrase Voltaire: Don't allow the perfect to be the enemy of the good.* Remember that an OKR can be modified or even scrapped at any point in its cycle. Sometimes the "right" key results surface weeks or months after a goal is put into play. OKRs are inherently works in progress, not commandments chiseled in stone.

A few goal-setting ground rules: Key results should be succinct, specific, and measurable. A mix of outputs and inputs is

---

* Or as Sheryl Sandberg says: "Done is better than perfect."

helpful. Finally, completion of all key results *must* result in attainment of the objective. If not, it's not an OKR.*

Table 4.2: An OKR Quality Continuum

Weak	Average	Strong
Objective: Win the Indy 500. **Key result:** Increase lap speed. **Key result:** Reduce pit stop time.	**Objective:** Win the Indy 500. **Key result:** Increase average lap speed by 2 percent. **Key result:** Reduce average pit stop time by one second.	**Objective:** Win the Indy 500. **Key result:** Increase average lap speed by 2 percent. **Key result:** Test at wind tunnel ten times. **Key result:** Reduce average pit stop time by one second. **Key result:** Reduce pit stop errors by 50 percent. **Key result:** Practice pit stops one hour per day.

Less Is More

As Steve Jobs understood, "Innovation means saying no to one thousand things." In most cases, the ideal number of quarterly OKRs will range between three and five. It may be tempting to usher more objectives inside the velvet rope, but it's generally a mistake. Too many objectives can blur our focus on what counts, or distract us into chasing the next shiny thing. At MyFitnessPal, the health and fitness app, "We were putting too much down,"

---

* For a more comprehensive manual, see "Google's OKR Playbook," in the resource section at the back of this book.

says CEO Mike Lee. "There were too many things we were trying to get done, and then the prioritization wasn't clear enough. So we decided to try to set fewer OKRs, and to make sure that the ones that really matter are the ones that we set."

For individuals, as I found out for myself at Intel, selective goal setting is the first line of defense against getting overextended. Once contributors have consulted with their managers and committed to their OKRs for the quarter, any add-on objectives or key results must fit into the established agenda. *How does the new goal stack up against my existing ones? Should something be dropped to make room for the new commitment?* In a high-functioning OKR system, top-down mandates to "just do more" are obsolete. Orders give way to questions, and to one question in particular: What matters most?

When it came to goal setting, Andy Grove felt strongly that less is more:

> The one thing an [OKR] system should provide par excellence is focus. This can only happen if we keep the number of objectives small. . . . Each time you make a commitment, you forfeit your chance to commit to something else. This, of course, is an inevitable, inescapable consequence of allocating any finite resource. People who plan have to have the guts, honesty, and discipline to drop projects as well as to initiate them, to shake their heads "no" as well as to smile "yes." . . . We must realize— and act on the realization—that if we try to focus on everything, we focus on nothing.

Above all, top-line objectives must be *significant.* OKRs are neither a catchall wish list nor the sum of a team's mundane tasks. They're a set of stringently curated goals that merit special attention and will move people forward in the here and now. They link to the larger purpose we're expected to deliver around. "The *art* of management," Grove wrote, "lies in the capacity to select from the many activities of seemingly comparable significance the one or two or three that provide leverage well beyond the others and concentrate on them."

Or as Larry Page would say, winning organizations need to "put more wood behind fewer arrows." That, in very few and focused words, is the essence of our first superpower.

5

Focus:
The Remind Story

Brett Kopf
Cofounder

I t's no news that the U.S. education system needs help. A Brown University study pointed to one possible solution: better communication between teachers and families. When summer school teachers made daily phone calls and sent texts or written messages home, their sixth-graders completed 42 percent more homework. Class participation rose by nearly half.

For decades, companies have tried to boost student achievement by injecting technology into schools. It hasn't worked. But suddenly, while nobody was looking, tens of millions of American kids walked into the classroom with a transformational piece of tech in their pockets. Thanks to the pervasive smartphone, text messaging became the leading mode of teenage communication. Remind found a market opportunity: to make texting a secure and practical communication system for principals, teachers, students, and parents.

Focus is essential for choosing the right goals—for winnowing

OKR wheat from chaff. Brett Kopf discovered the urgency of focus while building Remind, enabling teachers, students, and parents to text in a safe and secure environment. By using OKRs to zero in on its top priorities, the company is serving millions of people who matter for the future of this country.

When Brett and I first met, I was struck by his passion for serving his customers. His start-up was exquisitely focused on teachers. I'll never forget stepping into the bathroom of his tiny loft office and seeing a list of company objectives taped to the mirror, over the commode. Now *there* was a sign of serious goal orientation.

I found Brett highly skilled at identifying priorities and enlisting others to buy in. In 2012, he and his brother David made the *Forbes* honor roll of "30 Under 30 Education." But with accelerating scale, their company needed more focus. OKRs guaranteed a process that they'd already begun.

––––

Brett Kopf: Growing up in Skokie, Illinois, I struggled to focus at school. I was fine if I could move around, but sitting at a desk for me was torture. A forty-minute math lesson felt like eternity. I was the kid who was always messing with my neighbor or blowing spitballs. I just wasn't engaged.

I was tested in fifth grade, and then came the diagnosis: attention deficit hyperactivity disorder and dyslexia. Organizing words and letters was tough for me. Numbers were tougher still.

Both my parents were entrepreneurs, and I'd see them up and working at five in the morning. I was working my butt off, too, but my grades kept sinking and my confidence with them. It only got worse in high school, on the North Side of Chicago. When other kids called me stupid, I believed them.

Then, junior year, a teacher named Denise Whitefield began

working with me one-on-one—and changed my life. Each day she'd begin by asking, "What do you have to do today?" I'd run down my list: a history worksheet, an English essay, an upcoming math test. Then she'd say something really smart: "Okay, let's just pick one and talk about it." We focused on one thing at a time, and I'd get it done. "Just keep trying," she encouraged me. "You'll get it. I have all day." The panicked beating in my chest subsided. School would never be easy for me, but I began to believe I could handle it.

My mother spoke to Mrs. Whitefield every week, came into school at least once a month. They were a force in lockstep, Team Brett, and they would not let me fail. I'm sure I didn't fully get the importance of their connection, but it planted a seed.

Even after my grades improved, the college-prep ACT exam—*answer six hundred questions and don't move for four hours*—was a horror movie for a person with ADHD. But somehow I made it into Michigan State, my first big win.

When people try to crack the country's massive problems in education, they usually start with curriculum or "accountability," which is code for test scores. What gets lost are the human connections. That's what Remind is all about.

Twitter for Education

Like many ventures, Remind began with one person's problem. As a college freshman, I was hopeless with academic deadlines and schedules, which my professors seemed to change on a whim. Cut off from my support system, I failed at three majors before settling on agricultural economics, the easiest one I could find. But I still had five syllabi per semester, and each syllabus might contain thirty-five assignments and quizzes and tests. Success in college is a matter of time management. When to start writing that ten-page poli-sci essay? How to prep for the chem final? It's all about dynamic goal setting, and I kept dropping the ball.

Things came to a head junior year, after I slaved over an essay and got a mediocre grade. Adding insult, I had to hunt for that lousy grade on a clunky web-based system on my laptop. My friends and I texted on our BlackBerrys in real time—why couldn't our school data be at our fingertips, too? Why couldn't teachers connect with students on their smartphones anytime, anywhere? I felt driven to build something to help kids like me. I called my older brother, David, who was working in web services security for a big Chicago insurance firm. I said, "You have twenty-four hours to decide if you want to start that company with me." Five minutes later he called back and said, "Okay, I'm in."

For two years, David and I fumbled in the dark. We knew nothing about technology and less about product development or operations. (My total real-world experience was an internship at Kraft Foods, where I'd mostly stocked cookies.) Random students shared their syllabi, and I plugged them into David's Excel macros to send alerts to their phones: "Brett Kopf, you have a quiz at eight a.m. tomorrow in History 101, don't forget to study." The system was archaic and absolutely unscalable. But for a few hundred active users, including me, it worked. I graduated from Michigan State.

In early 2011, I moved to Chicago to work on our app full time. With $30,000 from friends and family, David and I did the full-monty entrepreneur thing, pasta dinners every night. And we failed because I was arrogant. We spent lots of time meeting potential investors and working up intricate website schematics, and no time learning about teachers' problems. We weren't yet focused on what counted.

Down to a few hundred dollars, our company cheated death by getting into Imagine K12, the Silicon Valley start-up accelerator for the education market. Our mission statement went something like: "Remind101: A safe way for teachers to message students and parents. We're building the most powerful communication platform in education and using SMS as the 'hook.' Think Twitter, for education." There were millions of children with learning issues like mine, and countless teachers struggling to help them. I was bold or naive enough to think we could do something about it.

With our Demo Day opportunity ninety days out, David quit his job and we moved to the Valley. We learned the three watchwords for entrepreneurs:

- Solve a problem
- Build a simple product
- Talk to your users

While David locked himself in a room to teach himself how to code, I focused on a single ten-week goal: to interview 200 teachers across the United States and Canada. (I guess you could say that was my first OKR.) After contacting 500 teachers on Twitter, I wound up with 250 one-on-ones, exceeding my objective. When you listen to enough educators in the trenches, you learn pretty quickly that off-site communication ranks high among their pain points. At final bell, teachers were plastering sticky notes— *Homework's due tomorrow*—on students' shoulders. Couldn't we do better than that?

Traditional phone trees and permission slips were labor intensive and unreliable. On the other hand, texting between thirty-year-old teachers and twelve-year-old children was loaded with liability. Teachers needed a secure platform with no personal data attached, something accessible yet private. And they needed *less* work, not more.

By Day 15, we had a crude beta version of Remind. On a sheet of printer paper, over hand-drawn symbols for mobile phones and email, I scrawled, "Your students can receive your messages. . . ." Below were three options: "Invite," "Print," "Share." After reaching a teacher on Skype, I'd hold the paper to the screen and say, "You can type any message you want to your students, hit the button, and they'll never see your phone number or social networking profile." I did this countless times, and the teachers just about fell out of their chairs—every time. "My God," they'd say, "that would solve such a big problem for me!"

That's when David and I knew we were on the right track.

Scaling on a Shoestring

By Day 70, our software was in place. Teachers could sign up on the web, form a virtual "class," and provide a dedicated number to students and parents for text messaging. We scaled quickly, a good sign—130,000 messages within three weeks of launch. We had what every new company wanted, a hockey-stick growth chart. On Demo Day, I entered a big, buzzing room with eleven other start-ups and a hundred investors. I had two minutes to make my pitch, followed by two hours of frantic mingling. I handed out my card to at least forty people.

Growth costs money. By early 2012, my brother and I were $10,000 in debt. But then Miriam Rivera and Clint Korver's Ulu Ventures seeded us with a save-the-day $30,000. Another infusion followed from Maneesh Arora, the Google product manager who later founded MightyText and became my mentor. Remind kept scaling like crazy on our seed-capital shoestring. Sometimes—most of the time—it felt like the sorcerer's apprentice, moving really fast and out of control. At one point we were adding eighty thousand users a day when we had five people, and only two of us were engineers. We'd yet to spend a dime on marketing. I spoke to teachers for feedback, and they'd put out the word to fifty colleagues. Since our service was free, we didn't need school district approval.

Our goals stayed strictly qualitative until the fall of 2013, when we hit six million users and raised Series A funding from Chamath Palihapitiya and the Social+Capital Partnership. Maneesh had already been nudging us to back our decisions with more data, and Chamath showed us how to paint a picture with one page of it. Plus he taught us to discern what was *inessential*, like our number of registered users. Nobody cared how many teachers registered on Remind if they never came back to use it.

By the time John Doerr saw our goals posted above our office toilet, they were more concrete. We listed three metrics: Weekly Active Teachers (WAT), Monthly Active Teachers (MAT), and retention.

Then I'd squeeze in a few quarterly initiatives: migrate the databases, build the app, hire four people. I wanted everyone in the company to see just what we were doing.

Working out of a one-bedroom loft, still plagued by a chronic shortage of engineers, we'd barely gotten our mobile app up and running. But John could tell we were homed in on what mattered. Our objectives were clear and quantified, and we were teacher-obsessed from the start.

In February 2014, just before we closed our Series B funding (led by Kleiner Perkins), John pitched us on OKRs. He told us about some companies using them: Intel, Google, LinkedIn, Twitter. Here

Remind cofounder Brett Kopf, Clintondale Community Schools coprincipals Meloney Cargill and Dawn Sanchez, Remind cofounder David Kopf, 2012.

was a method to keep us focused, to guide and track and support us at every step. And I thought: Why not try it?

Goals for Growth

That August, the heart of our busy back-to-school season, the Remind app exploded: more than 300,000 student and parent downloads per day. We were number three in the Apple App Store! By the end of the fall semester, we'd passed the billion-message mark. Our operation had to ramp up in a hurry, in each and every department.

None of our goal setting was glamorous, but all of it was very necessary.

We started OKRs when our company had fourteen people. Within two years, we'd grown to sixty. We couldn't all meet around a table anymore to hash out the next quarter's priorities. OKRs helped enormously by helping people to focus on what could move the company to the next level. To meet our objective for teacher engagement, with its time-bound key result, we had to defer many other things. In my view, you can only do one big thing at a time really well, and so you better know what that one thing is.

OBJECTIVE

Support company hiring.

KEY RESULTS

1. Hire 1 director of finance and operations (talk to at least 3 candidates).
2. Source 1 product marketing manager (meet with 5 candidates this quarter).
3. Source 1 product manager (meet with 5 candidates this quarter).

For example: To this day, one of our most requested features is a repeated message. Say a teacher wants to remind a fifth-grade class to bring the novel they're reading to school—and keep reminding them every Monday morning without resending. That's a classic "delight" feature, but was it worth the engineering time to make it a top-line priority? Would it move the needle for user engagement? When our answer was *no*, we decided to shelve it—a tough call for a teacher-centric organization. Without our new goal-setting discipline and focus, we might not have held our ground.

OKRs gave us a way to move forward that wasn't all top-down. After voting on the quarter's top objectives, the leadership team would go to our contributors and say, "Here's what we think is important and why." And the contributors would say, "Okay, how do we get there?" Since it was all written down, everybody knew what everyone else was doing. There was no confusion or Monday-morning quarterbacking. OKRs took politics out of play.

The system helped my personal focus, too. I tried to limit myself to three or four individual objectives, tops. I printed them out and kept them close on my notepad and next to my computer, every-where I went. Each morning, I'd say to myself, "These are my three buckets, and what am I doing today to move the company forward?" That's a great question for any leader, with or without a learning issue.

I was wide open about my progress or lack of it. I'd tell my peo-ple, "Here are the three things I'm working on, and I'm failing at this one miserably." As companies scale, people need to see the CEO's priorities and how they can align for maximum impact. And they need to see it's okay to make a mistake, to correct it and move on. You can't fear screwing up. That squelches innovation.

At a fast-growing start-up, effective leaders keep firing them-selves from jobs they did at the beginning. Like many founders, I handled accounting and payroll, which drained a lot of time. One of my first OKRs was to offload the financial tasks and focus on prod-uct and strategy, our big-picture objectives. Meanwhile, I had to adjust to working through a layer of executives. My OKRs smoothed the transition and made it stick. They kept me from backsliding or micromanaging.

An OKR Legacy

OKRs are basically simple, but you don't master the process off the bat. Early on, we'd be off by miles in our company-level objectives, mostly on the way-too-ambitious side. We might set seven or eight of them when we had the capacity for two, at best.

When John entered our lives, I was new to strategic planning. We probably should have eased into OKRs more slowly and not installed the whole system at once. But whatever our mistakes, I'd do it again in a heartbeat. OKRs helped Remind become a better-managed company, a company that executes. Three quarters after our first implementation, we secured $40 million in Series C funding. Our future was assured.

———

The sky's the limit for Remind. Through all its growth and changes, it has never lost sight of its core constituency, those hard-working teachers. Brett and David Kopf are unwavering in their vision "to give every student an opportunity to succeed." As Brett says: We live in a time when you can click a button and get a cab within five minutes. But when a child lags in school, it can take weeks or months for a parent to find out about it. Remind is on its way to solving that problem—by focusing on what matters.

6

Commit:
The Nuna Story

Jini Kim

Cofounder and CEO

Nuna is the story of the passionate Jini Kim, propelled by family tragedy to deliver better health care to huge numbers of Americans. Of how she bootstrapped Nuna through years of rejection. And of how she recruited engineers and data scientists to commit to a wildly audacious goal: building a new Medicaid data platform, from scratch.

Alongside focus, commitment is a core element of our first superpower. In implementing OKRs, leaders must publicly commit to their objectives and stay steadfast. At Nuna, a health care data platform and analytics company, the cofounders overcame a false start with OKRs. They went on to clarify priorities for the entire organization. They realized that they needed to show a sustained commitment to reach their own individual OKRs, and to help their team do the same.

Nuna took off in 2014. Four years and one enormous Medicaid contract later, the company is leveraging data to make the health care system work better for millions of people who need it most.

Applying the technology and lessons learned from its Medicaid work, Nuna is helping large companies improve the efficiency and quality of care in their private plans. All of this work is supported by the goal-setting prowess of OKRs, which Jini first encountered as a Google product manager.

This story reflects two aspects of our commitment superpower. Once Nuna's team got the hang of them, OKRs locked in their commitment to their highest-impact goals. At the same time, both leaders and contributors learned to commit to the OKR process itself.

———

Jini Kim: The story of Nuna is very personal. When my brother Kimong was two years old, he was diagnosed with severe autism. A few years later, he had his first grand mal seizure at Disneyland. One second he was fine, and the next he was on the floor, barely able to breathe. As Korean immigrants with limited resources and little English, my parents felt helpless. Without a safety net, my family would surely have gone bankrupt. The task of signing us up for Medicaid fell to me, at age nine.

When I joined Google in 2004, my first job out of college, I'd never heard of OKRs. But over time, they became an indispensable compass to help me and my teams navigate through Google and get the most important work done. One of the first products I worked on, Google Health, taught me the importance of data for improving health care. I also learned just how difficult it can be to gain access to health care data, even one's own. In 2010, that experience led me to found Nuna.

We didn't use OKRs in the beginning. Nuna had no money and no customers. I was working full time and five others part time (including my grad student cofounder, David Chen), but no one was getting paid. We stitched together a prototype and talked to some large self-

Nuna CEO Jini Kim with brother Kimong.

insured employers. That first year we got zero orders, and rightfully so. We thought we knew what the market needed, but we didn't yet understand our customers well enough to effectively advocate for the product.

When we still had no orders in year two, I knew it was time to get an education. What did benefits directors actually care about? What did meaningful innovation look like in the health care market? I put on a suit and crashed some human resources conferences to find out.

In 2012, the things I'd learned helped us sign some Fortune 500 companies as clients. More than two years of rejection, frustration, and more ramen dinners than I could count had finally led Nuna to a product-market fit. But at a start-up, the only constant is change, and Nuna was about to undergo a dramatic one. After I returned to the Bay Area from a six-month stint with Healthcare.gov, we closed

$30 million of funding. We'd finally be able to pay our team, and for many years to come.

By that point, I'd learned of a government request-for-proposals to build the first-ever database for all Medicaid members: 74.5 million lives in fifty states, five territories, and the District of Columbia. The effort had already failed multiple times. After seventy-two hours fueled by adrenaline and Red Bull, we submitted our bid just on time to the Centers for Medicare & Medicaid Services (CMS). Two months after that, we found out we had won the contract.

Scaling Nuna was an enormous undertaking, in three dimensions. The first was the business itself, to upgrade compliance, security, and privacy. The second was our data platform infrastructure. The third was our employee base, from fifteen people to seventy-five. We'd have to construct a historic database while still running our existing employer business—and to finish within a year. To deliver, we'd need more focus and commitment than ever before.

In 2015, we made an initial try to implement OKRs. As an ex-Googler, I was sold on the power of objectives and key results. But I underestimated what it took to introduce them, much less to execute them effectively. You need to build your goal muscle gradually, incrementally. As I know too well from my own private wellness OKR to run a marathon: Doing too much too soon will definitely end in pain.

We created quarterly OKRs and annual OKRs, and rolled them out to everybody at Nuna from day one. We were tiny then, around twenty people—not such a big lift, you might think. But the process didn't take. Some people never set their individual OKRs; others set them, but stuck them in a drawer.

With hindsight, I would have started with our leadership team of five. For structured goal setting to prosper, as our company learned the hard way, executives need to commit to the process. It may take a quarter or two to overcome your managers' resistance and get them acclimated to OKRs—to view them not as a necessary evil, or some perfunctory exercise, but as a practical tool to fulfill your organization's top priorities.

Until your executives are fully on board, you can't expect contributors to follow suit—especially when a company's OKRs are aspirational. The more challenging an objective, the more tempting it may be to abandon it. People naturally look to their bosses in setting goals and following through. If the officers jump ship in the middle of a stormy voyage, you can't expect the sailors to bring it into port.

In mid-2016, we tried again, with a renewed level of OKR commitment. But even as I saw our executive team buy in, I knew I couldn't be complacent. As the leader, it was my job to keep after people. I would email our contributors to commit to creating individual OKRs. If they didn't respond, I would reach out to them via Slack, the team messaging app. If they still didn't hear me, I would text them. And if they *still* didn't listen, I would grab them and say, *"Please* do your OKRs!"

To inspire true commitment, leaders must practice what they teach. They must model the behavior they expect of others. After sharing my individual OKRs at an all-hands meeting, I was surprised by just how much it helped the company rally around the process. It showed everyone that I, too, was accountable. Our contributors feel free to evaluate my OKRs and tell me how to improve them, which has made all the difference. Here's one example, with my grades (on the Google scale of 0.0 to 1.0) in brackets. I can tell you that I received a lot of constructive input in formulating this deceptively simple and make-or-break hiring OKR:

OBJECTIVE

Continue to build a world-class team.

KEY RESULTS

1. Recruit 10 engineers [0.8].
2. Hire commercial sales leader [1.0].
3. One hundred percent of candidates feel they had a well-organized, professional experience even if Nuna does not extend an offer [0.5].

We also added two key results to measure our commitment to professional development:

OBJECTIVE

Create a healthy and productive work environment as we scale to more than 150 employees.

KEY RESULTS

1. One hundred percent of Nunas have gone through performance review/feedback cycle [1.0].
2. One hundred percent of Nunas score their individual Q3 OKRs within the first week of Q4 [0.4].

At Nuna, our commitment to OKRs is very public and visible. But there are times when the system is more useful in a private mode. In the fourth quarter of 2016, I set my sights on hiring a VP for our employer business, a critical step to accelerate the growth of that business unit. It was a new position for the company, and I was unsure how it would be perceived internally. Establishing a private OKR, for which only David and I were accountable, deepened my commitment to get the hiring process moving. It pushed me to speak one-on-one to key stakeholders in the company, find potential recruits, and finally set into motion a more formal recruitment process.

By definition, start-ups wrestle with ambiguity. As Nuna's terrain has expanded, from self-insured employers to the massive Medicaid database to a suite of new health plan products, we've come to rely on OKRs more than ever. Our whole team needs sharper focus and clearer priorities, the prerequisites for deeper commitment. OKRs have forced a bunch of conversations in the company that otherwise would not have happened. We're getting more alignment. Instead of reacting to external events on the fly, we're acting purposefully on our plans for each quarter. Our deadlines are stricter, yet they also feel more attainable. We're *committed* to doing what we've said we will do.

What's the moral of our OKR story? As David says, "You're not going to get the system just right the first time around. It's not going to be perfect the second or third time, either. But don't get discouraged. Persevere. You need to adapt it and make it your own." Commitment feeds on itself. Stay the course with OKRs, as I know firsthand, and you will reap amazing benefits.

Today, with the invaluable support of our CMS partners, Nuna has built a secure, flexible data platform to store private health information for more than 74 million Americans. But we aspire to do so much more. We want our platform to inform policy makers as they grapple with governing a costly and complex health care system. We want it to drive analytics, to help predict and prevent future ailments. Most of all, we want it to play a big role in improving the nation's health care. It's a daunting commitment. But as I learned at Google: The hairier the mission, the more important your OKRs.

All these years later, my little brother Kimong speaks only three words: *uhma*, *appa*, and *nuna*—Korean for mom, dad, and big sister. Kimong gave our company both its name and its mission. Now it's up to us, backed by our commitment to OKRs, to help improve health care for everyone.

———

In January 2017, Nuna peeled back the curtain on its Medicaid work. Interviewed by *The New York Times*, Andrew M. Slavitt, acting director of the Centers for Medicare & Medicaid Services, described Nuna's cloud database as "near historic," a leap from state-level computing silos to the first "systemwide view across the program."

In just a few short years, Nuna's team has made a lasting impact on the U.S. health care system. But anyone who knows Jini and David—and the strength of their commitment to OKRs—will tell you they are just getting started.

7

Superpower #2:
Align and Connect for
Teamwork

We don't hire smart people to
tell them what to do.
We hire smart people so they can
tell us what to do.

—*Steve Jobs*

With the eruption of social media, transparency is the default setting for our daily lives. It's the express lane to operating excellence. Yet at most companies today, goals remain secrets. Too many CEOs share the frustration of Aaron Levie, founder and CEO of Box, the enterprise cloud company. "At any given time," Aaron said, "some significant percentage of people are working on the wrong things. The challenge is knowing which ones."

Research shows that public goals are more likely to be attained than goals held in private. Simply flipping the switch to "open" lifts achievement across the board. In a recent survey of one thousand working U.S. adults, 92 percent said they'd be more motivated to reach their goals if colleagues could see their progress.

In an OKR system, the most junior staff can look at everyone's goals, on up to the CEO. Critiques and corrections are out in public view. Contributors have carte blanche to weigh in, even on flaws in the goal-setting process itself. Meritocracy flourishes in sunlight. When people write down "This is what I'm working on," it's easier to see where the best ideas are coming from. Soon it's apparent that the individuals moving up are the ones doing what the company most values. Organizational poisons—suspicion, sandbagging, politicking—lose their toxic power. If sales hates the latest marketing plan, they won't be simmering inside their silo; their differences will be aired out in the open. OKRs make objectives *objective*, in black and white.

Transparency seeds collaboration. Say Employee A is struggling to reach a quarterly objective. Because she has publicly tracked her progress, colleagues can see she needs help. They jump in, posting comments and offering support. The work improves. Equally important, work relationships are deepened, even transformed.

In larger organizations, it's common to find several people unwittingly working on the same thing. By clearing a line of sight to everyone's objectives, OKRs expose redundant efforts and save time and money.

The Same Page

Once top-line objectives are set, the real work begins. As they shift from planning to execution, managers and contributors alike tie their day-to-day activities to the organization's vision. The term for this linkage is *alignment,* and its value cannot be overstated. According to the *Harvard Business Review,* companies with highly aligned employees are more than twice as likely to be top performers.

Unfortunately, alignment is rare. Studies suggest that only 7 percent of employees "fully understand their company's business strategies and what's expected of them in order to help achieve the common goals." A lack of alignment, according to a poll of global CEOs, is the number-one obstacle between strategy and execution.

"We've got a lot of stuff going on," says Amelia Merrill, an HR leader at RMS, a California risk modeling agency. "We've got people in multiple offices in multiple time zones—some doing parallel work, some doing work together. And it's really hard for employees to see what they should work on first. Everything seems important; everything seems urgent. But what *really* needs to get done?"

The answer lies in focused, transparent OKRs. They knit each individual's work to team efforts, departmental projects, and the overall mission. As a species, we crave connection. In the workplace, we're naturally curious about what our leaders are doing and how our work weaves into theirs. OKRs are the vehicle of choice for vertical alignment.

The Grand Cascade

In the bygone business world, work was strictly driven from the top. Goals were handed down the org chart like tablets from Mount Sinai. Senior executives set top-line objectives for their department heads, who passed them to the next tier of management, and so on down the line.

While this approach to goal-setting is no longer universal, it remains prevalent at most larger organizations. The appeal is obvious. Cascaded goals corral lower-level employees and guarantee that they're working on the company's chief concerns. In the best case, cascading forges unity; it makes plain that we're all in this together.

In my pitch to Google and many other organizations, I've used an imaginary football team to show how the OKR system works effectively—or not—when used in this fashion.

Follow along as we cascade a set of OKRs from top to bottom.

The Sand Hill Unicorns: Fantasy Football

Let's say I'm the general manager of the Sand Hill Unicorns. I have one objective, the *WHAT*: Make money for the owner.

General Manager

OBJECTIVE
Make $ for owner.
KEY RESULTS
1. Win Super Bowl.
2. Fill home stands to 90%+.

OKR Chart 1—General Manager

My objective has two key results: win the Super Bowl and fill the stands to at least 90 percent capacity, which is *HOW* I will make money for the owner. If I fulfill both of those *HOWs*, there is no way we can fail to show a profit. So it's a well-constructed OKR.

> **With our top-level OKRs set, we work our way down the organization.**

Head Coach

OBJECTIVE

Win Super Bowl.

KEY RESULTS

1. Passing attack amasses 300+ yards per game.
2. Defense allows fewer than 17 points per game.
3. Special teams unit ranks in top 3 in punt return coverage.

Offensive Coach

OBJECTIVE

Generate 300-yards-per-game passing attack.

KEY RESULTS

1. Achieve 65% pass completion rate.
2. Cut interceptions to fewer than 1 per game.
3. Hire new quarterbacks coach.

Defensive Coach

OBJECTIVE

Give up fewer than 17 points a game

KEY RESULTS

1. Allow fewer than 100 rushing yards per game.
2. Increase number of sacks to 3+ per game.
3. Develop a Pro Bowl cornerback.

Special Teams Coach

OBJECTIVE

Improve to top 3 ranking for punt coverage team.

KEY RESULTS

1. Allow fewer than 10 yards per punt return.
2. Block 4+ punts over the season.

OKR Chart 2 — Coaches

As general manager, I cascade my goal down to the next level of management, the head coach and the senior vice president of marketing. My key results become their objectives. (See OKR Chart 2.) The head coach's objective is to win the Super Bowl, with three key results to get him there: a passing attack of at least 300 yards per game, a defense surrendering fewer than seventeen points per game, and a top three ranking in punt return coverage. He cascades those KRs as objectives for his top three executives, the offensive and defensive coordinators and special teams coach. They in turn devise their own, lower-level key results. To achieve a 300-yards-per-game passing attack, for example, the offensive coordinator might aim for a 65 percent pass completion rate and less than one interception per game—after hiring a new quarterbacks coach.

> These OKRs are aligned to the general manager's aim to win the Super Bowl.

> We are not done yet. We need to define how we'll fill up our home stands.

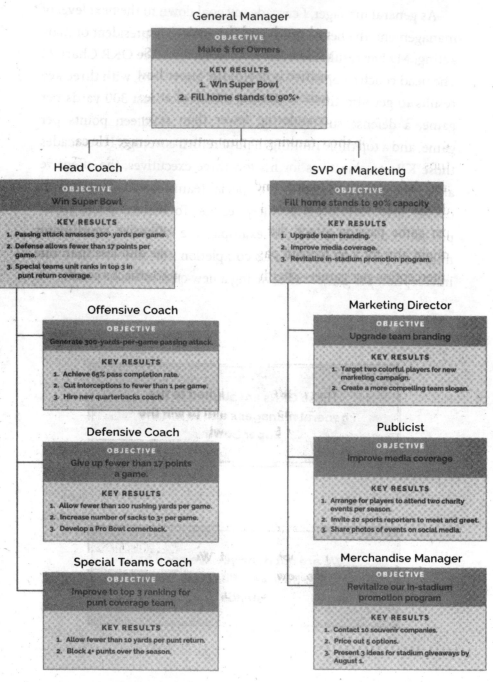

OKR Chart 3—OKRs for the Organization

Meanwhile, my SVP of marketing has derived *her* objective from my other key result, to fill the stands to 90 percent capacity. (See OKR Chart 3.) She's crafted three key results: Upgrade the team's branding, improve our media coverage, and revitalize the in-stadium promotion program. These KRs are cascaded as objectives for the marketing director, team publicist, and merchandise manager, respectively.

Now, what's wrong with this picture? Here's a clue: The SVP's key results are a mess. Unlike the head coach's KRs, they're unmeasurable. They're not specific or time bound. How do we define "improvement," for example, in the team's media coverage? (Five special features on ESPN? One cover spread in *Sports Illustrated*? Fifty percent more followers on social media?)

But even if the SVP came up with stronger key results, the organization's goal-setting approach would remain deeply flawed. The top-line objective—to make a wealthy person wealthier—lacks intrinsic motivation for the general manager, much less for the team's East Coast scout or the PR intern slaving away at the copy machine.

In moderation, cascading makes an operation more coherent. But when *all* objectives are cascaded, the process can degrade into a mechanical, color-by-numbers exercise, with four adverse effects:

- *A loss of agility.* Even medium-size companies can have six or seven reporting levels. As everyone waits for the waterfall to trickle down from above, and meetings and reviews sprout like weeds, each goal cycle can take weeks or even months to administer. Tightly cascading organizations tend to resist fast and frequent goal setting. Implementation is so cumbersome that quarterly OKRs may prove impractical.

- *A lack of flexibility.* Since it takes so much effort to formulate cascaded goals, people are reluctant to revise them mid-cycle. Even minor updates can burden those downstream, who are scrambling to keep their goals aligned. Over time, the system grows onerous to maintain.

- *Marginalized contributors.* Rigidly cascaded systems tend to shut out input from frontline employees. In a top-down ecosystem, contributors will hesitate to share goal-related concerns or promising ideas.

- *One-dimensional linkages.* While cascading locks in vertical alignment, it's less effective in connecting peers horizontally, across departmental lines.

Bottoms Up!

Fortunately, we have an alternative. Precisely because OKRs are transparent, they can be shared without cascading them in lockstep. If it serves the larger purpose, multiple levels of hierarchy can be skipped over. Rather than laddering down from the CEO to a VP to a director to a manager (and then to the manager's reports), an objective might jump from the CEO straight to a manager, or from a director to an individual contributor. Or the company's leadership might present its OKRs to everyone at once and trust people to say, "Okay, now I see where we're going, and I'll adapt my goals to that."

Considering that Google has tens of thousands of employees, its innovative culture would be hamstrung by OKRs cascaded by rote. As Laszlo Bock, a former head of the company's People Operations, observes in *Work Rules!*:

Having goals improves performance. Spending hours cascading goals up and down the company, however, does not. . . . We have a market-based approach, where over time our goals all converge because the top OKRs are known and everyone else's OKRs are visible. Teams that are grossly out of alignment stand out, and the few major initiatives that touch everyone are easy enough to manage directly.

The antithesis of cascading might be Google's "20 percent time," which frees engineers to work on side projects for the equivalent of one day per week. By liberating some of the sharpest minds in captivity, Google has changed the world as we know it. In 2001, the young Paul Buchheit initiated a 20 percent project with the code name *Caribou.* It's now known as Gmail, the world's leading web-based email service.

To avoid compulsive, soul-killing overalignment, healthy organizations encourage some goals to emerge from the bottom up. Say the Sand Hill Unicorns' physical therapist attends a sports medicine conference and learns of a new regimen for injury prevention. Of her own volition, she coins an off-season OKR to implement the therapy. Her objective may not align with her direct manager's OKRs, but it aligns with the general manager's overarching objective. If the Unicorns' top players stay healthy through the season, the team's chances of winning the Super Bowl will soar.

Innovation tends to dwell less at the center of an organization than at its edges. The most powerful OKRs typically stem from insights outside the C-suite. As Andy Grove observed, "People in the trenches are usually in touch with impending changes early. Salespeople understand shifting customer demands before management does; financial analysts are the earliest to know when the fundamentals of a business change."

Micromanagement is mismanagement. A healthy OKR environment strikes a balance between alignment and autonomy, common purpose and creative latitude. The "professional employee," Peter Drucker wrote, "needs rigorous performance standards and high goals. . . . But how he does his work should always be his responsibility and his decision." At Intel, Grove took a dim view of "managerial meddling": "[T]he subordinate will begin to take a much more restricted view of what is expected of him, showing less initiative in solving his own problems and referring them instead to his [or her] supervisor. . . . [T]he output of the organization will consequently be reduced. . . ."

An optimal OKR system frees contributors to set at least some of their own objectives and most or all of their key results. People are led to stretch above and beyond, to set more ambitious targets and achieve more of those they set: "The higher the goals, the higher the performance." People who choose their destination will own a deeper awareness of what it takes to get there.

When our *how* is defined by others, the goal won't engage us to the same degree. If my doctor orders me to lower my blood pressure by training for the San Francisco Marathon, I might grudgingly take it under advisement. But if I decide of my own free will to run the race, I'm far more likely to reach the finish line— especially if I'm running with friends.

In business, I have found, there is rarely a single right answer. By loosening the reins and backing people to find *their* right answers, we help everybody win. High-functioning teams thrive on a creative tension between top-down and bottom-up goal setting, a mix of aligned and unaligned OKRs. In times of operational urgency, when simple *doing* takes precedence, organizations may choose to be more directive. But when the numbers are strong and a company has grown too cautious and buttoned-up, a lighter touch may be just right. When leaders are attuned to the fluctuating needs of both the business and their employees, the mix of top-down and bottom-up goals generally settles at around half-and-half. Which sounds about right to me.

Cross-functional Coordination

Even as modern goal setting successfully transcends the org chart, unacknowledged dependencies remain the number one cause of project slippage. The cure is lateral, cross-functional connectivity, peer-to-peer and team-to-team. For innovation and advanced problem solving, isolated individuals cannot match a connected group. Product relies on engineering, marketing on sales. As business becomes more intricate and initiatives more complex, interdependent divisions need a tool to help them reach the finish line together.

Connected companies are quicker companies. To grab a competitive advantage, both leaders and contributors need to link up horizontally, breaking through barriers. A transparent OKR system, as Laszlo Bock points out, promotes this sort of freewheeling collaboration: "People across the whole organization can see what's going on. Suddenly you have people who are designing a handset reaching out to another team doing software, because they saw an interesting thing you could do with the user interface."

When goals are public and visible to all, a "team of teams" can attack trouble spots wherever they surface. Adds Bock: "You can see immediately if somebody's hitting the ball out of the park—you investigate. If somebody's missing all the time, you investigate. Transparency creates very clear signals for everyone. You kick off virtuous cycles that reinforce your ability to actually get your work done. And the management tax is zero—it's amazing."

8

Align:
The MyFitnessPal Story

Mike Lee
Cofounder and CEO

It all started with a beach wedding. Heading into their nuptials, Mike and Amy Lee wanted to lose some weight. A fitness trainer gave them a list of the nutritional values of three thousand foods—and a pad of paper for tracking calories. Mike, who'd programmed computers since the age of ten, knew there had to be a better way. So he conceived a solution, which became MyFitnessPal. For eight years, Mike and Albert self-funded the app from savings and credit cards.

Today, the brothers Lee are at the center of an epic movement for quantitative, self-digital health and personal well-being. Their mission is to create a healthy planet. In 2013, when Kleiner Perkins invested in MyFitnessPal, the app had 45 million registered users. Today it has more than 120 million, and they've lost a collective 300 million pounds. With a database of 14 million foods plus real-time links to Fitbit and dozens of other apps, MyFitnessPal makes it easier than ever to track what you eat and how effectively you exercise. By revealing what used to be hidden—

the calories you burn on your morning run, for example—MyFitnessPal helps users set and achieve ambitious personal goals. Members make daily choices that change their lives. As a bonus, the app comes with a network of friends who cheer you on each day.

OKRs are not islands. To the contrary, they create networks—vertical, horizontal, diagonal—to connect an organization's most vital work. When employees align with a company's top-line goals, their impact is amplified. They stop duplicating efforts or working counterproductively against the grain. As brothers Mike and Albert Lee discovered while building MyFitnessPal, the world's leading health and fitness app, strong alignment is critical to the day-to-day progress that kindles the next big leap.

If this story sounds like a perfect setting for OKRs, you're not mistaken. Goal setting came organically for Mike and Albert—though not always easily, as you will see. In February 2015, their company was acquired by Under Armour for $475 million. The merger married MyFitnessPal's strength in technology to one of the industry's great brands. Suddenly the Lees had access to world-class professional athletes, the next frontier for digital fitness. As Mike says, "We want to skate to where the puck is going."

The new business structure brought new challenges for goal setting, around alignment in particular. Mike and Albert would rely on OKRs to navigate a labyrinth of internal relationships. As MyFitnessPal dove into a much larger pond, objectives and key results would align its growing team and their goals.

———

Mike Lee: You have a device in your pocket that's incredibly powerful. The data it collects—on yourself and the world around you—is exploding. For a nominal cost or none at all, you can have a coach or a nutritionist or even a medical consultant on hand at all times. Thanks to our smartphones, we can make healthier decisions and lead healthier lifestyles.

MyFitnessPal provides insights—we call them "moments of clarity"—that stick with our users all their lives. I know firsthand that it works. When I first began tracking what I ate, I learned that mayonnaise has ninety calories per tablespoon, and mustard only five. I haven't touched a drop of mayo since. Make enough of those small changes, and you'll find they add up.

I worked for a number of companies before cofounding MyFitnessPal. None of them used formal goal-setting systems. They had annual financial plans, revenue numbers to hit, and broad strategies around them, but nothing structured or continuous. Not coincidentally, those organizations shared something else in common: a glaring lack of alignment. I'd have no clue as to what other teams were doing, or how we might work together toward a common objective. We'd try to compensate with more meetings, which only wasted time. If you put two people in a boat and have one row east and the other row west, they'll use up lots of energy going nowhere.

In our early days at MyFitnessPal, we'd joke that we had a thousand-item to-do list, and we'd cross off the top three items and say, "Okay, *that* was a good year." We left a lot below the line, but that was okay. We worked within our limits: launch the Android app, or the BlackBerry app, or the iPhone or iPad version. We tackled one goal at a time and worked until it was done, and then we moved to the next item on the list. Rarely was there overlap.

Our process wasn't sophisticated, but it was focused and highly measurable. When you're defining a company's strategy on your own, with just one other person working on products, alignment is simple. My brother and I would declare a keystone goal—*launch on the iPad by such-and-such a date*—and communicate each day on our progress. Small organizations can get by with less process. Though now I wish we'd had our OKRs in gear earlier on, even before we got funded. We'd have been better prepared to make sounder choices when opportunity came our way.

Once MyFitnessPal got up and running on the iPhone and Android, our growth shot off the charts. One day we woke up and had 35 million registered users. We were scaling too fast to do one thing at a time anymore. I found that entropy begins when you have two great people directly under you. You want to give each of them something big and purposeful to work on, and they both naturally want to move their piece of the project, and soon they're pulling out of alignment and charging in different directions. Before you

MyFitnessPal cofounders Mike and Albert Lee, 2012.

know it, they're working on two different things. It doesn't help to push them harder. If two nails are even slightly misaligned, a good hammer will splay them sideways.

Though Albert and I knew we needed more structure in our goal setting, we weren't certain how to proceed. In 2013, not long after Kleiner Perkins first invested in our company, John Doerr came by to pitch us on OKRs. His football team analogy resonated with me; I just *got* it. I loved the simplicity of the main objective, and the way it was distilled and stretched and cascaded through the organization. And I thought to myself: *That* was how we'd get our company aligned.

Cross-team Integration

When we began to implement OKRs, it was harder than anticipated. We didn't appreciate how much thought it took to create the right company objectives, and then to cascade them down to drive contributors' behavior. We found it challenging to strike a balance between high-level, strategic thinking and more granular, directive communication. Once we had our Series A funding and scaled up our leadership team, our realm of the possible expanded. In a push for accountability, we set one big dedicated goal for each leader. We created company OKRs for people instead of matching people to our OKRs—we had it backward. Some objectives were too narrow, others too nebulous. If an HR manager got stuck trying to connect to the high-level goals for product or revenue, we'd add a top-line objective just for that person. Soon we had a cornucopia of company OKRs, but what really *mattered* at MyFitnessPal? We'd lost the forest for the trees.

In 2013, as we jumped from ten to thirty people, I assumed we'd become 200 percent more productive. I'd underestimated how much scaling slows you down. New engineers need extensive training before they can be as proficient as your holdovers. And with multiple engineers developing the same project, we had to build new processes to keep them from overriding one another. In the transition, productivity took a hit.

When you come down to it, alignment is about helping people understand what you want them to do. Most contributors will be motivated to ladder up to the top-line OKRs—assuming they know where to set the ladder. As our team got larger and more layered, we confronted new issues. One product manager was working on Premium, the enhanced subscription version of our app. Another focused on our API platform, to enable third parties like Fitbit to connect to MyFitnessPal and write data to it or applications on top of it. The third addressed our core login experience. All three had individual OKRs for what they hoped to accomplish—so far, so good.

The problem was our shared engineering team, which got caught in the middle. The engineers weren't aligned with the product managers' objectives. They had their own infrastructure OKRs, to keep the plumbing going and the lights on. We assumed they could do it all—a big mistake. They got confused about what they should be working on, which could change without notice. (Sometimes it boiled down to which product manager yelled loudest.) As the engineers switched between projects from week to week, their efficiency dragged. When returning to a product after an interruption, they'd have to ask themselves: How does this go again? The Premium work was especially urgent for revenue, yet it went in fits and starts.

I felt super-frustrated. We'd hired all these talented people and were spending tons of money, but we weren't going any faster. Things came to a head over a top-priority marketing OKR for personalized emails with targeted content. The objective was well constructed: We wanted to drive a certain minimum number of monthly active users to our blog. One important key result was to increase our click-through rate from emails. The catch was that no one in marketing had thought to inform engineering, which had already set its own priorities that quarter. Without buy-in from the engineers, the OKR was doomed before it started. Even worse, Albert and I didn't find out it was doomed until our quarterly postmortem. (The project got done a quarter late.)

That was our wake-up call, when we saw the need for more alignment between teams. Our OKRs were well crafted, but implementation fell short. When departments counted on one another for crucial support, we failed to make the dependency explicit. Coordination was hit-and-miss, with deadlines blown on a regular basis. We had no shortage of objectives, but our teams kept wandering away from one another.

The following year, we tried to fix the problem with periodic integration meetings for the executive team. Each quarter our department heads presented their goals and identified dependencies. No one left the room until we'd answered some basic questions: Are we meeting everyone's needs for buy-in? Is a team overstretched? If so, how can we make their objectives more realistic?

Alignment doesn't mean redundancy. At MyFitnessPal, every OKR has a single owner, with other teams linking up as needed. As I see it, co-ownership weakens accountability. If an OKR fails, I don't want two people blaming each other. Even when two or more teams have parallel objectives, their key results should be distinct.

Each time we went through the OKR process, we did a little better. Our objectives got more precise, our key results more measurable, our achievement rate higher. It took us two or three quarters to really get the hang of it, particularly for product features keyed to a broad objective. It's not easy to predict the market for the conceptually new; we'd wildly beat our metric or wildly miss. So we switched it up. We began pinning our key results to deadlines instead of revenue or projected users. (Example: "Launch MFP Premium by 5/1/15.") After a feature launched and some real data came back, we'd be in a stronger position to assess its impact and potential. Then our next round of OKRs could be more realistically keyed (or stretched) to projected outputs.

At times we'd see our team choosing lower-risk key results, like sending emails here or push notifications there. The more ambitious the stretch in the objective, the more conservatively people made their KRs—a classic unintended consequence. So we learned to design our goals to fit the context. Where appropriate, we went for the incremental. But there were times when we told the team, "Don't worry about monthly active user impact on this one. Just build the best feature you can. We want you to swing for the fences."

Unacknowledged Dependencies, Writ Larger

Going with Under Armour meant adapting to a company with a whole different mode of goal setting. Suddenly I had a boss to align with and a newly formed division to run: UA Connected Fitness–North America. Our mandate was to leverage emerging digital technologies to improve fitness and performance. I had three additional apps to coordinate, each with a different culture and working style.

At scale, alignment grows exponentially more complex. How would we show four hundred people what we were trying to achieve, to help them align with us and with one another? How could we get everybody rowing in the same direction? In the beginning, I found it really hard to do; I can hardly imagine how Amazon or Apple manages. When we introduced OKRs throughout our division, it made a big difference.

A few weeks after our acquisition, my boss called an off-site leadership meeting for twenty people, including Connected Fitness stakeholders across the company. Since Under Armour followed an annual cadence, department heads were to present what they aimed to achieve that year. At MyFitnessPal, we were accustomed to investing the time to frame our objectives correctly. Our group was ready.

As the meeting unfolded, Albert and I were surprised to discover that the ecommerce team was counting on us to drive significant traffic from our apps. The data team assumed we'd deliver a mass of data. The media sales team had marked us down for a set dollar amount in new ad revenues. All three had preconceived notions of what they could expect from us, with no visibility into what other teams were asking. Nor could anyone see how their targets might align with our own growth objectives, much less the bigger company picture. There were unacknowledged dependencies wherever we looked. It was our old problem at MyFitnessPal, on steroids. There was simply no way we could get all these things done.

It took eighteen months to straighten out our division's alignment, and we couldn't have done it without OKRs. First, we had to define our capacity constraints for developing new software. Then we had to clarify our core priorities. By sharing our high-level OKRs for Connected Fitness, I could explain why certain projects required the allocated time, and where we should be doubling down on the company's top goals. "This is the process we use," I

98

said, "and I'm showing you our objectives and key results. You need to let me know if you see anything missing, or if you think we're working on the wrong things."

It was one-way transparency, and I felt a little nervous going in, but it worked. People began to recognize our limits and adjust their expectations accordingly. For our part, we worked to align with them by finding projects that met cross-departmental objectives.

When Albert took hold of our MapMyFitness product team, first he examined the road map and said, "We need to cut half of this, right? We need to strip it down to the things that really matter." Now we evaluate product features the MyFitnessPal way: "If we take this one off the road map this quarter, what happens? Would it really affect the user experience?" More often than not, the feature in question wouldn't make a big difference. These calls are not subjective; we have metrics to measure impact. We're making tougher, sharper choices about where to place our bets these days, and they all stem from the OKR process.

Focus and alignment are binary stars. In May 2015, three months after Under Armour acquired us, our Premium subscription version finally launched. It couldn't happen until we openly admitted, "Look, we can't get all of these things done. We have to choose." We had to make it clear to the company that Premium was our number-one objective, above all else.

We're still a work in progress. Shortly after the merger, two of our four apps simultaneously implemented maps inside their run-tracking functions. Because they'd failed to collaborate in development, they built their maps in different ways with different providers. Beyond the obvious inefficiency, our customers' experience would be inconsistent. To their credit, the two teams devised a monthly check-in to avoid similar problems in the future. Shortly thereafter, we implemented OKRs throughout the division. Now we're all on the same page. Everyone knows our group's top priorities, which gives them freedom to say no to other things.

North Star Alignment

Though our start-up days are behind us, we're still ambitious goal setters. We still stand by our OKR values of transparency and accountability. We publish our objectives on a wiki that anybody in the company can see. We discuss them at weekly all-hands meetings. At a recent off-site retreat, I demonstrated our OKR process to the larger leadership group—and they just ate it up. "Best off-site we've ever had," one executive said. With OKRs entrenched as the operational foundation for Connected Fitness, my hope is to spread them by example throughout Under Armour. The larger the organization, the more value the system offers.

Beyond making objectives more consistent within a company, alignment contains a deeper meaning. It's about keeping your goals true to your North Star values. Connected Fitness is deliberately aligned with Under Armour's mission "to make all athletes better." At the same time, we still live by the old MyFitnessPal mantra: *When our customers succeed at reaching their health and fitness goals, we succeed as a company.* As a team, we're still posing the question that Albert and I asked each other at the beginning: Will this feature—or this partnership—help our customers succeed?

After all, it's our users who do the hard work to change their lives. Like the woman who rose from her chair without using her hands, for the first time in twenty years—a poignant moment of clarity. To the extent we've succeeded as a company, it's in helping to provide those moments. Whenever possible, we spell this out in our high-level objectives, as you can see in the following OKR from a few years back:

OBJECTIVE
Help more people around the world

KEY RESULTS

1. Add 27M new users in 2014.
2. Reach 80M total registered users.

Every decision we make needs to square with our vision. When we face a trade-off between our customers and a business goal, we align with the customer. When an objective seems out of line with our mantra, it gets extra scrutiny. Before moving forward, we make sure it lines up with our North Star. That's what keeps us walking the walk and connected with the people we serve. That's what makes us who we are.

9

Connect:
The Intuit Story

Atticus Tysen

Chief Information Officer

ntuit has made *Fortune*'s prestigious list of the "World's Most Admired Companies" for fourteen years running. The firm made its first splash in the 1980s with Quicken, which brought personal finance to the desktop computer and became a household name. Then came tax preparation software (TurboTax) and a desktop accounting program (QuickBooks), which eventually moved online. Over its long history, by tech standards, Intuit has survived one competitive threat after the next by staying a step ahead. Most recently, it sold Quicken and reconstructed QuickBooks Online as an open platform. Subscriptions soared by 49 percent. "Whenever Intuit makes a wrong turn," UBS analyst Brent Thill told *The New York Times*, "they quickly get off the gravel and back onto the blacktop. That's why the company has done so well for such a long time."

People can't connect with what they cannot see; networks

cannot blossom in silos. By definition, OKRs are open and visible to all parts of an organization, to each level of every department. As a result, companies that stick with them become more coherent.

Adaptable organizations tend to be more openly connected ones. Intuit's culture of transparency was ingrained by cofounder

Intuit CIO Atticus Tysen at Goal Summit, 2017.

Scott Cook and strengthened by "Coach" Bill Campbell, who served as Intuit's CEO and longtime chairman. "Bill was one of the most open guys I've ever met," says Atticus Tysen, Intuit's senior vice president and chief information officer. "He could read people and he invested in them. You always knew what he was thinking and that he was in your corner."

The Coach's legacy lives on. A few years ago, to help the IT department adapt as Intuit moved to the cloud, Atticus introduced OKRs to his direct reports. The following quarter, he rolled the system down to the director level; the quarter after that, to all six hundred IT employees. He was determined not to force the new process. "We didn't want bureaucratic compliance," Atticus says. "We wanted enthusiastic compliance. I wanted to see if the OKR system would succeed on its own—and it really did."

Each quarter, Intuit's IT group tackles about 2,500 active objectives. As they've built their goal-setting muscle with real-time, automated data and routine check-ins, users align roughly half of their OKRs with the goals of higher-ups or their department. Collectively, they view their managers' OKRs more than four thousand times per quarter, or seven views per employee—a strong marker of frontline engagement. After the Lasik surgery of OKRs, contributors see clearer links between their own day-to-day work, their colleagues' priorities, their team's quarterly objectives, and the company's "True North" mission.

Intuit's story demonstrates the benefits of an OKR pilot project before (or even without) a full-company rollout. A few hundred users may suffice for an OKR laboratory, to iron out any kinks before deployment at scale. At Intuit, says CEO Brad Smith, who posts his own goals in his office for anyone to see, connected goal setting "is critical to enabling employees to do the best work of their lives."

—

Atticus Tysen: I'd been working at Intuit for eleven years on the product side before moving to the IT department. Then, in 2013, I became CIO. I made the switch because I loved the company, and I knew IT needed to evolve to help Intuit on its new mission. It was a stressful, exciting time. The organization was pivoting in several directions at once: from desktop software to cloud-based software, from a closed platform to one that was open to thousands of third-party apps, from a North American company to a global company. As we leaned into our long-term strategy to become an integrated ecosystem, we gradually changed from a house of brands (TurboTax, Quicken, Quick-Books) to the branded house of Intuit.

In the storm of any disruption, IT will bear the brunt of in-house frustrations. Partly it's because the operation tends to be opaque. Any thirty-plus-year-old company accumulates layers of complex technology—especially a technology company. In IT, we're always juggling the needs of internal partners with the demands of our end users. We bridge technology and business outcomes. Maybe toughest of all, we must balance the task of making systems work perfectly today (as our people expect) with our mandate to invest in the future. For example: Intuit used to have nine different billing systems to serve our array of products, and each of them had special challenges. When you're putting out fires every day, it's hard to build a next-generation billing technology.

How could we signal to our workforce what mattered most while keeping them all up and running? And how could we assure all hands that we had their concerns covered? In a conventionally siloed organization, activity is opaque. People might try to look into what's going on outside their own department, but they often don't know where to start or have the time to follow up.

At Intuit, change started at the top. To jump-start our transformation, our chairman and CEO, Brad Smith, installed a company-wide goal-setting system. Brad is very conscious and intentional about this. Once each month, managers meet with their reports to discuss individual goals. The system has built-in, 360-degree feedback, with both parties comparing notes on a regular basis.

Our company has a long cultural history around learning and experimentation. We try a lot of things, keep the elements that work best, and adapt them to make them our own. I agreed to partner with HR to try OKRs in Enterprise Business Solutions, or EBS (our moniker for IT). Back in 2014, I first discovered objectives and key results while Googling "goal setting." My research suggested that OKRs might help us change the way we operate, even how we perceive ourselves.

Modern IT goes way beyond checking off boxes to process help tickets or change requests. It's about adding *value* to the business—shedding redundant clone systems, creating new functionality, finding future-oriented solutions. To become the team Intuit needed, our EBS would need to change root and branch. Our leaders had to give people air cover to back-burner some day-to-day tasks and focus on more valuable, longer-term initiatives.

Today, every employee in my department owns three to five business objectives per quarter, along with one or two personal ones. The system is powerful precisely because it is so simple— and so transparent. For our OKRs to be effective, I knew they'd have to be visible through all of Intuit, even if no one outside EBS used them. I wanted everyone in the company to know exactly what we were doing, and how, and why. When people understand your priorities and constraints, they're more apt to trust you when something goes sideways.

Early on, I found it challenging to separate my individual goals from the department's OKRs. As IT's leader, I thought they should logically coincide. But it wasn't a good optic. Most of our top-level objectives endured from quarter to quarter, typically for eighteen months. Down the line, teams and individuals would modify their own OKRs as the environment shifted and we kept making progress. And they were asking, quite reasonably, "What is the CIO doing if his goals never change?" I got the message. Now I have my own objectives, and I ladder up to our top-level OKRs like everyone else.

Beyond our base in the Bay Area, we made it a point to implement the system worldwide. EBS has formal teams in four U.S. regions and in Bangalore, the high-tech center of southern India, plus support teams in every Intuit location around the globe. When people work outside the center, they're left to wonder what gets done at headquarters. (And headquarters may wonder about them, too.) OKRs ended the mystery. They made us more cohesive; they brought us together.

One of our top-level EBS objectives is to "rationalize, modernize, and secure all technology used to run Intuit." (See page 108.) Lately, whenever I travel to see a team in Texas or Arizona, I hear our people saying, "This project is rationalizing our portfolio." Or: "How can we modernize that system?" No matter where they happen to be stationed, they're using the same three verbs. When a new project comes up for discussion, they'll ask one another how it fits into our OKR template. If it doesn't, they'll rightly raise a red flag: "Why are we doing this?"

> **OBJECTIVE**
>
> Modernize, rationalize, and secure the technology used to run the business of Intuit.
>
> **KEY RESULTS**
>
> 1. Complete migration of Oracle eBusiness Suite to R12 and retire 11.5.9 this quarter.
> 2. Deliver wholesale billing as a platform capability by end FY16.
> 3. Complete onboarding of agents in small business unit to Salesforce.
> 4. Create a retirement plan for all legacy technology.
> 5. Draft and get alignment on new Workforce Technology strategies, road maps, and principles.

Live Data from the Cloud

Intuit views itself as a thirty-four-year-old start-up. Beginning with the personal computer in the 1980s, our history reflects a series of tech disruptions, with each new platform upending its predecessor. Our first product was on DOS. Then we moved to Windows and Macintosh on the desktop, then to mobile devices, and most recently to the cloud.

OKRs can be deployed to even greater effect in the cloud era. Horizontal alignment comes naturally. With open, public goal setting, the data and analytics team could see from the start what our financial systems team had in mind. It was immediately obvious that they should be working together, in parallel. The teams linked up their objectives in real time, rather than after the fact—a sea change from our historical way of doing things.

At a desktop software company, leaders look at operations through a twentieth-century retail lens. They postmortem sales reports and channel flow. While they do their best to predict where the business might be headed, their line of sight is largely limited to the rearview mirror. By contrast, a cloud-based business wants to know what is happening *now*. How many subscriptions came in this week? How many trials are ongoing? What's our conversion rate? A customer can Google an online product, skim the marketing page, take it for a spin, and make a purchase—all in ten minutes or less. For leaders to keep pace, they should be checking their funnel on a daily basis. At EBS, we need to be thinking about real-time reporting, data, and analytics, even as we build out features like wholesale billing. We've captured this necessity in a top-level objective:

OBJECTIVE

Enable every Intuit worker to make decisions based on "live" data.

KEY RESULTS

1. Deliver functional data marts for HR and Sales.
2. Complete migration to new Enterprise Data Warehouse built for real-time access.
3. Create single team operating all data visualization tools across Intuit to drive a unified strategy.
4. Create teaching module to help people in other teams use data visualization tools.

A Tool for Global Collaboration

As Intuit becomes more global, asynchronous collaboration is increasingly a way of life. When we're working from headquarters with our team in Bangalore, live video has limited utility. Given the thirteen-hour time difference, our associates in India will be sleeping when we're working, and vice versa. Three years ago, there were few practical options. Intuit invested in the latest workplace tools, but we lacked solutions for persistent chat, collaborative authoring, and videoconferencing. People were forced to improvise, with uneven results. Productivity slipped.

To attack the problem in a more connected way, we upgraded a key result for workforce technology to its own top-level OKR. In the space of six months, our new strategic emphasis led us to add several new tools, all integrated into a single authentication system: Slack for persistent chat, Google Docs for collaborative editing, Box for content management, BlueJeans for next-wave video technology. Our open OKR platform helped teams across EBS to make the transition and align with our new top-line objective. Now our people can focus on their work instead of wasting time to figure out which tool to use.

There's an art to goal setting, and more than a few judgment calls. If you choose to temporarily elevate a key result, it helps to be candid about it. Leaders need to explain, "Yes, I want us to focus on that one right now as a top-level objective. When it no longer needs the extra attention, we'll let it drift back down into a KR." It's a dynamic system. You're always adjusting the altitude.

> ## OBJECTIVE
> Deliver awesome end-to-end workforce technology solutions and strategies.
>
> ### KEY RESULTS
> 1. Implement Box pilot for first 100 users by mid-quarter.
> 2. Complete BlueJeans rollout to final users by end of the quarter.
> 3. Transfer first 50 individual account Google users to enterprise account by end of the quarter.
> 4. Finalize Slack contract by end of month 1 and complete rollout play by end of the quarter.

———

Studies have told us forever that frontline employees thrive when they can see how their work aligns to the company's overall goals. I've found this especially true at our remote sites. I've heard it from people in Bangalore: "My objective is directly a key result of my manager's OKR, which ties directly to the top-level EBS objective, which ties to the company's shift to the cloud. Now I understand how what I'm doing in India connects to the company mission." That's a powerful realization. OKRs have consolidated our far-flung department. Thanks to structured, visible goal setting, our boundaries have melted away.

Horizontal Connections

Intuit was a flat organization from the start, with just a handful of tiers between the CEO and frontline employees. Our founder, Scott

Cook, believed the best idea should win, not the biggest title, and that still holds true today. From the day I came in as a group manager, I was impressed by the collaborative culture. Even when we ran things in silos, we were vertically open. You could always speak freely to your manager, or your manager's manager, and get a respectful hearing.

OKRs have opened our department *horizontally*, across teams. At first it was awkward. Everybody in IT instinctively wanted to align with their managers' goals—or with mine. I went into the platform one day and found literally hundreds of key results linked to one of my top-level objectives. I told people, "Your manager is still your manager. You'll continue to collaborate—none of that's going to change. But you need to disconnect from us and connect to each other."

Our ecommerce and billing teams work under separate vice presidents who roll up to me. If ecommerce is building a shopping cart, billing needs to bring related features to market. In the old way, the two engineering teams ran independently and reported to their respective program managers, who tried (with variable success) to connect from above. The people doing the actual work had no direct contact.

Now, with horizontally transparent OKRs, our engineers intentionally connect as they link to each other's objectives. Quarter by quarter, they iterate against the department's objectives while devising how best to coordinate with their peers. We're trending away from senior committee mandates and toward real autonomy. Our EBS leaders still set the context, ask the big questions, and furnish relevant data. But it's our interconnected groups whose insights are propelling us forward—together.

10

Superpower #3:
Track for Accountability

In God we trust; all others must bring data.

—W. Edwards Deming

One underrated virtue of OKRs is that they can be *tracked*—and then revised or *adapted* as circumstances dictate. Unlike traditional, frozen, "set them and forget them" business goals, OKRs are living, breathing organisms. Their life cycle unfolds in three phases, which I'll consider in turn.

The Setup

While general-purpose software can get an OKR process up and running, there's a catch: It doesn't scale. When one Fortune 500 company recently tried to ramp up its goal-setting cadence, it hit a wall. All of its 82,000 contributors had dutifully recorded their annual objectives in Microsoft Word files! A move to quarterly OKRs would have generated 328,000 files per year. They'd all be public, in theory, but who would have the patience to search out connections or alignment? If you share a goal that nobody sees, is the system truly transparent?

In 2014, when Bill Pence came to AOL as global chief technology officer, top-line company and division goals were presented on a spreadsheet and rolled down from there. "But they never really had a home, where they connected on a daily basis with people," Pence says. Without frequent status updates, goals slide into irrelevance; the gap between plan and reality widens by the day. At quarter's end (or worse, year's end), we're left with zombie OKRs, on-paper *whats* and *hows* devoid of life or meaning.

Contributors are most engaged when they can actually see how their work contributes to the company's success. Quarter to quarter, day to day, they look for tangible measures of their achievement. Extrinsic rewards—the year-end bonus check—merely validate what they already know. OKRs speak to something more powerful, the intrinsic value of the work itself.

As the bar for structured goal setting rises, more organizations are adopting robust, dedicated, cloud-based OKR management software. The best-in-class platforms feature mobile apps, automatic updating, analytics reporting tools, real-time alerts, and integration with Salesforce, JIRA, and Zendesk. With three or four clicks, users can navigate a digital dashboard to create, track, edit, and score their OKRs. These platforms deliver transformative OKR values:

- *They make everyone's goals more visible.* Users gain seamless access to OKRs for their boss, their direct reports, and the organization at large.

- *They drive engagement.* When you know you're working on the right things, it's easier to stay motivated.

- *They promote internal networking.* A transparent platform steers individuals to colleagues with shared professional interests.

- *They save time, money, and frustration.* In conventional goal setting, hours are wasted digging for documentation in meeting notes, emails, Word documents, and PowerPoint slides. With an OKR management platform, all relevant information is ready when you are.

At AOL, CEO Tim Armstrong felt the company's goals were "too disconnected," Bill Pence recalls. "They weren't linked together; they didn't cascade up and down. They just didn't stay tethered to the employees and the work they were doing through the year." In 2016, Armstrong brought in a dedicated platform and rolled out OKRs. The upshot, Pence says, was radical transparency, real-time connection, and a company that coordinated operations as a matter of course.

OKR Shepherd

For an OKR system to function effectively, the team deploying it—whether a group of top executives or an entire organization—must adopt it universally. No exceptions, no opt-outs. Yes, there will be late adopters, resisters, and garden-variety procrastinators. To prod them to join the flock, a best practice is to designate one or more OKR shepherds. For years, that role in Google's products department was filled by senior vice president Jonathan Rosenberg. Here is one of Jonathan's classic communiqués, with the laggards' names deleted to protect the guilty:

From: Jonathan Rosenberg

Date: Thu, Aug 5, 2010 at 2:59 PM

Subject: Amidst boundless opportunities, 13 PMs whiff on OKRs (names included)

Product Gang,

As most of you know, I strongly believe that having a good set of quarterly OKRs is an important part of being successful at Google. That's why I regularly send you notes reminding you to get them done on time, and why I ask managers to review them to make sure all of our OKRs are good. I've tried notes that are nice and notes that are mean. Personal favorites include threatening you with Jonathan's Pit of Despair in October 07 and celebrating near perfection in July 08. Over time I iterated this carrot/stick approach until we reached near 100% compliance. Yay!

So then I stopped sending notes, and look what happened: this quarter, SEVERAL of you didn't get your OKRs done on time, and several others didn't grade your Q2 OKRs. It turns out it's not the type of note I send that matters, but the fact that I send anything at all! Names of the fallen are duly noted below (with a pass given to several AdMob employees who are new to the ways of Google, and to many of you who missed the deadline but still got them done in July).

We have so many great opportunities before us (search, ads, display, YouTube, Android, enterprise, local, commerce, Chrome, TV, mobile, social . . .) that if you can't come up with OKRs that get you excited about coming to work every day, then something must be wrong. In fact, if that's really the case, come see me.

In the meantime, please do your OKRs on time, grade your previous quarter's OKRs, do a good job at it, and post them so that the OKR link from your moma [intranet] page works. This is not administrative busywork, it's an important way to set your priorities for the quarter and ensure that we're all working together.

Jonathan

Midlife Tracking

As the Fitbit craze attests, people crave to know how they're progressing and see it visually represented, down to the percentage point. Research suggests that making measured headway can be more incentivizing than public recognition, monetary inducements, or even achieving the goal itself. Daniel Pink, the author of *Drive*, agrees: "The single greatest motivator is 'making progress in one's work.' The days that people make progress are the days they feel most motivated and engaged."

Most goal management platforms use visual aids to show progress toward objectives and key results. Unlike steps on Fitbit, OKRs don't require daily tracking. But regular check-ins—preferably weekly—are essential to prevent slippage. As Peter Drucker observed, "Without an action plan, the executive becomes a prisoner of events. And without check-ins to reexamine the plan as events unfold, the executive has no way of knowing which events really matter and which are only noise."

As noted in chapter 4, the simple act of writing down a goal increases your chances of reaching it. Your odds are better still if you monitor progress while sharing the goal with colleagues—two integral OKR features. In one California study, people who recorded their goals *and* sent weekly progress reports to a friend attained 43 percent more of their objectives than those who merely thought about goals without sharing them.

OKRs are adaptable by nature. They're meant to be guardrails, not chains or blinders. As we track and audit our OKRs, we have four options at any point in the cycle:

- *Continue*: If a green zone ("on track") goal isn't broken, don't fix it.

- *Update*: Modify a yellow zone ("needs attention") key result or objective to respond to changes in the workflow or external environment. What could be done differently to get the goal on track? Does it need a revised time line? Do we back-burner other initiatives to free up resources for this one?

- *Start*: Launch a new OKR mid-cycle, whenever the need arises.

- *Stop*: When a red zone ("at risk") goal has outlived its usefulness, the best solution may be to drop it.*

The point of a real-time dashboard is to quantify progress against a target and flag what needs attention. While OKRs are primarily a positive force for *more*, they also stop us from persisting in the wrong direction. As Stephen Covey noted, "If the ladder is not leaning against the right wall, every step we take just gets us to the wrong place faster." Late-in-game surprises are less likely when you track your OKRs for continuous feedback. Good news or bad, reality intrudes. In the process, "people can learn from failure and move on, perhaps turning some aspect of the setback into the seedling of a new success."

When Remind's school-messaging platform prototyped the company's first revenue-yielding service, a peer-to-peer payment system, it was a total flop. "No one used it," says Brett Kopf. "It didn't solve a clear problem. We immediately altered the goal to

---

* Usually this will apply to a key result, or *how* you're going about something. A thoughtfully set objective is less likely to implode within ninety days.

build an event-driven system, where the teacher could say, 'I've got a field trip next week. Are you coming, yes or no? And do you want to pay?' That changed everything. It started driving and growing like crazy."

Whenever a key result or objective becomes obsolete or impractical, feel free to end it midstream. There's no need to hold stubbornly to an outdated projection—strike it from your list and move on. Our goals are servants to our purpose, not the other way around.

One proviso: When an objective gets dropped before the end of the OKR interval, it's important to notify everyone depending on it. Then comes reflection: *What did I learn that I didn't foresee at the beginning of the quarter?* And: *How will I apply this lesson in the future?*

For best results, OKRs are scrutinized several times per quarter by contributors and their managers. Progress is reported, obstacles identified, key results refined. On top of these one-on-ones, teams and departments hold regular meetings to evaluate progress toward shared objectives. Whenever a committed OKR is failing, a rescue plan is devised. At Google, the frequency of team check-ins varies with the business needs of the moment, the gap between predicted outcomes and execution, the quality of intragroup communication, and the group's size and location(s). The more dispersed the team's members, the more frequently they touch base. Google's benchmark check-in cycle is monthly, at a minimum, though goal discussions there are so pervasive that formal meetings sometimes go by the boards.

Wrap-up: Rinse and Repeat

OKRs do not expire with completion of the work. As in any data-driven system, tremendous value can be gained from post hoc evaluation and analysis. In both one-on-ones and team meetings, these wrap-ups consist of three parts: objective scoring, subjective self-assessment, and reflection.

Scoring

In scoring our OKRs, we mark what we've achieved and address how we might do it differently next time. A low score forces reassessment: Is the objective still worth pursuing? If so, what can we change to achieve it?

On state-of-the-art goal management platforms, OKR scores are system-generated; the numbers are objective, untouched by human hands. (With less automated, homegrown platforms, users may need to perform their own calculations.) The simplest, cleanest way to score an objective is by averaging the percentage completion rates of its associated key results. Google uses a scale of 0 to 1.0:

- 0.7 to 1.0 = green.* (We delivered.)

- 0.4 to 0.6 = yellow. (We made progress, but fell short of completion.)

- 0.0 to 0.3 = red. (We failed to make real progress.)

---

* Google's floor of 0.7 for successful attainment reflects the high ambition of their "stretch" goals. (See chapter 12.) This threshold does not apply to the company's committed operational goals. For sales targets or product releases, any score under 1.0 would be deemed a failure.

Intel followed a similar formula. You may recall the OKR for Operation Crush, the company's push to reclaim the microprocessor market. Here are Andy Grove's actual marching orders from Q2 1980, as endorsed by his executive team (with end-of-quarter grades in brackets):

CORPORATE OBJECTIVE

Establish the 8086 as the highest-Performance 16-bit microprocessor family, as measured by:

KEY RESULTS (Q2 1980)

1. Develop and publish five benchmarks showing superior 8086 family performance [0.6].
2. Repackage the entire 8086 family of products [1.0].
3. Get the 8MHz part into production [0].
4. Sample the arithmetic coprocessor no later than June 15 [0.9].

And here is how these scores were determined:

- We completed three of five benchmarks for an 0.6, a borderline green.

- We did indeed repackage the 8086 family, under a new product line called iAPX. So that's a perfect 1.0.

- Production of the 8MHz part, set for early May, was a fiasco.* Because of problems with the polysilicon, the target had to be pushed to October. That's a zero.

---

* This KR reflects the awesome, compounding power of Moore's law. Eight megahertz was blazing speed at the time, but today you can buy a $300 Chromebook that runs better than two *giga*hertz—250 times faster.

- As for the arithmetic coprocessor, the goal was to ship 500 parts by June 15. We wound up shipping 470—which computes to 0.9, another green.

Altogether, we averaged 62.5 percent (or a raw score of 0.625) on our KRs for this objective, a respectable grade. The Intel board judged it below expectations but not too far below, because they knew how aggressively management set our goals. As a rule, we'd enter a quarter knowing we wouldn't achieve all of them. If a department so much as approached 100 percent, it was presumed to be setting its sights too low—and there would be hell to pay.

Self-assessment

In evaluating OKR performance, objective data is enhanced by the goal setter's thoughtful, subjective judgment. For any given goal in a given quarter, there may be extenuating circumstances. A weak showing by the numbers might hide a strong effort; a strong one could be artificially inflated.

Say the team's objective is to recruit new customers, and your individual key result is fifty phone calls. You wind up calling thirty-five prospects, for a raw goal score of 70 percent. Did you succeed or fail? By itself, the data doesn't afford us much insight. But if a dozen of your calls lasted several hours apiece and resulted in eight new customers, you might give yourself a perfect 1.0. Conversely: If you procrastinated, rushed through all fifty calls, and signed only one new customer, you might assess your performance at 0.25—because you could have pushed harder. (And on reflection: Should the key result have prioritized new customers, rather than calls?)

Or say you're a public relations manager, and your team's key result is to place three national articles about your company. Though you get only two pieces published, one is a cover story in *The Wall Street Journal*. Your raw score is 67 percent, but you say, "I'm giving us a 9 out of 10, because we hit that one out of the park."

Googlers are encouraged to use their OKRs in self-assessments—as guides, not as grades. As Shona Brown, former SVP of business operations, explained it to me, "It wasn't that they got a red or yellow or green, but here was a list of what they'd delivered on that was above business as usual and connected to the overall goals of the company." The point of objectives and key results, after all, is to get everyone working on the right things.

Table 10.1: Scoring and Assessment Variations

OKR	Progress	Score	Self-assessment
Bring in ten new customers.	70%	0.9	Due to a slump in the market, the OKR was significantly tougher to achieve than I'd thought. Our seven new customers represented an exceptionally good effort and outcome.
Bring in ten new customers.	100%	0.7	When I reached the objective only eight weeks into the quarter, I realized I'd set the OKR too low.
Bring in ten new customers.	80%	0.6	While I signed eight new customers, it was more luck than hard work. One customer brought in five others behind her.
Bring in ten new customers.	90%	0.5	Though I managed to land nine new customers, I discovered that seven would bring in little revenue.

Invariably, some people will grade themselves too harshly; others may need to be challenged. In either case, an alert facilitator or team leader will jump in and help recalibrate. In the end, the numbers are probably less important than contextual feedback and a broader discussion within the team.

Where OKR scores pinpoint what went right or wrong in the work, and how the team might improve, self-assessments drive a superior goal-setting *process* for the next quarter. There are no judgments, only learnings.

Reflection

OKRs are inherently action oriented. But when action is relentless and unceasing, it can be a hamster wheel of grim striving. In my view, the key to satisfaction is to set aggressive goals, achieve most of them, pause to reflect on the achievement, and *then* repeat the cycle. Learning "from direct experience," a Harvard Business School study found, "can be more effective if coupled with reflection—that is, the intentional attempt to synthesize, abstract, and articulate the key lessons taught by experience." The philosopher and educator John Dewey went a step further: "We do not learn from experience . . . we learn from reflecting on experience."

Here are some reflections for closing out an OKR cycle:

- Did I accomplish all of my objectives? If so, what contributed to my success?

- If not, what obstacles did I encounter?

- If I were to rewrite a goal achieved in full, what would I change?

- What have I learned that might alter my approach to the next cycle's OKRs?

OKR wrap-ups are retrospective and forward-looking at the same time. An unfinished objective might be rolled over to the next quarter, with a fresh set of key results—or perhaps its moment has passed, and it is appropriately dropped. Either way, sound management judgment comes first.

And one more thing. After thoroughly appraising your work and owning up to any shortfalls, take a breath to savor your progress. Throw a party with the team to celebrate your growing OKR superpowers. You've earned it.

11

Track:
The Gates Foundation Story

Bill Gates
Cochairman

Patty Stonesifer
Former CEO

I n 2000, the newly hatched Bill & Melinda Gates Foundation became something the world had never seen: a $20 billion start-up. Though Bill Gates had recently stepped down as CEO of Microsoft, he was still the company's chairman and chief product strategist. He had to find a way to channel the foundation's vast ambition, adapt to fluid conditions in the field, and allow himself—the extremely busy, famously fast-moving founder—to make the best possible choices. The higher the stakes, the more important it is to track progress—to flag looming problems, double back from dead ends, and modify goals on the run.

The newborn institution had signed on for the most audacious mission imaginable: "Everyone deserves a healthy and productive life." So its leaders enlisted scores of brilliant people who'd devoted their lives to global health and told them, "Quit thinking about incremental progress. What would you do if you had un-limited resources?"

By 2002, the foundation had scaled to the point where it ur-gently required a more structured form of goal setting. After CEO Patty Stonesifer heard my OKR pitch at an Amazon board meet-ing, she asked me to present it to the foundation. The rest is OKR history.

————

Patty Stonesifer: We had the beautiful gift of a blank sheet of paper: "How do you want to change the world?" But the gift also had a huge weight to it. Because when you have that big of a goal, how can you know you're making progress?

Melinda Gates, Patty Stonesifer, and Bill Gates reviewing OKRs, 2005.

We felt driven to be responsible with the capital. Bill and Melinda wanted to know that a disciplined system was in place to direct our hard choices. We borrowed from Jim Collins: "What can you be the best at in the world?" Once we figured that out, we laid the OKR system on top of it. We believed that everyone should have a healthy and productive life, and Bill and Melinda were passionate about the role of technology in creating change. That was in our DNA.

For a time we used a global health metric called Disability-Adjusted Life Years, or DALY. It gave us a data-driven framework for key results—say, to measure the impact of an investment in micronutrients against one to fight river blindness. DALY led us to focus on vaccines, which make such an enormous difference in productive life years. Now we had a credible metric, reinforced by our key results. OKRs made it all so clear.

———

Bill Gates: Ambitious, directional goals were always super-important at Microsoft. It was natural, in a way, because from a very young age I thought software was magic. In those early days, the exponential increase in transistors actually mapped to the performance of the device. We understood what the chips people were going to give us and that there was no end in sight, and that the storage and communication people likewise were writing exponential code. The screen people weren't quite as exponential, but the graphical user interface would be fast enough. There was only one missing element: the magic software to make the device do something interesting. I gave up on being a lawyer or a scientist, surefire things, because the idea of what would happen with all that intelligence—what I called "information at your fingertips"—was just so fascinating. It was mind-blowing to me.

Even before Paul Allen and I started the partnership, we were saying: *A computer on every desk and in every home.* IBM and other people—with resources and skill sets way beyond ours—weren't aiming for that goal. They didn't see it as a possibility, so they weren't pushing as hard to make it a reality. But we could see that it would happen. Moore's law would make things cheaper and get the software industry to critical mass. Those were big, big goals, and they started early for us.

That was our biggest advantage: We aimed higher.

Making Goals Concrete

In the year 2000, Melinda and I put $20 billion into the Gates Foundation. Suddenly it's both a start-up and the biggest foundation in the world. And the way the payout rules work, it has to spend a minimum of a billion dollars a year.

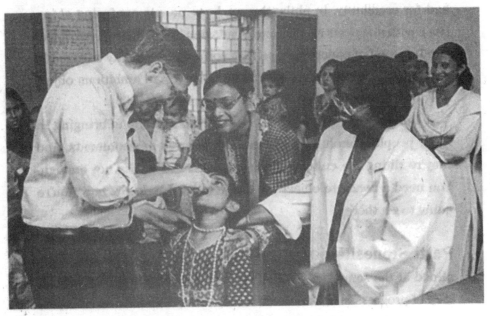

Bill Gates administering an oral polio vaccine
to a child in Mumbai, India, 2000.

I'd watched Andy Grove manage people on subgoals [key results], and I watched the Japanese, and I learned how you deal with things when people fall short. I don't think I invented anything there, but I did watch and learn. Then Patty Stonesifer brought in OKRs, the green-yellow-red approach, and it worked. When we used OKRs with our grant reviews, I felt good about what we were going after. I was still running Microsoft, and my time was limited, and Patty had to make things very efficient between us, to make sure we agreed. The goals process was a big part of that. There were two cases where I turned down a grant in the end because the goals weren't clear enough. The OKR system made me confident I was making the right call.

I'm a huge fan of goals, but they need to be handled correctly. At one point, the malaria team thought we'd eradicate the disease by 2015, which wasn't realistic. When a goal is too aspirational, it's bad for credibility. In philanthropy, I see people confusing *objectives* with *missions* all the time. A mission is directional. An objective has a set of concrete steps that you're intentionally engaged in and actually trying to go for. It's fine to have an ambitious objective, but how do you scale it? How do you measure it?

I think it's getting better, though. Philanthropy is bringing in more people from high-performance business environments, and they're tilting the culture. Having a good mission is not enough. You need a concrete objective, and you need to know how you're going to get there.

———

Patti Stonesifer: OKRs allowed us to be ambitious and disciplined at the same time. When measurable key results revealed a lack of progress or showed that an objective was unachievable, we reallocated the capital. If the goal was to eliminate Guinea worm disease, a very ambitious top-line goal, it was important to know whether the dollars and resources were making progress against it. With OKRs, we could set both quarterly and annual beats for substantial key results against such a huge objective.*

Until you set a really big goal, like vaccinating every child everywhere, you can't find out which lever or mix of levers is most important. Our annual strategy reviews began with: "What is the objective here? Is it eradication or is it expanding the reach of vaccines?" Then we could get more practical with our key results— like the 80/90 rule at the Global Alliance for Vaccines and Immunization, where 80 percent of districts would have 90 percent or more coverage. You need those key results to align your everyday activities, and over time you keep moving them to be even more ambitious against that really big goal.

Sometimes, to be honest, we were probably measuring the wrong thing. But the effort was always there to hold ourselves accountable. At private foundations, where you lack a market effect to gauge impact, you have to pay close attention to whether your data is getting you to the ultimate goal. We were learning so fast that sometimes we had to change data sets midstream. Say you had a seed that would double production of yams, and you were focused on that number. But then it turned out that nobody would use the seed because the yams took four times longer to cook at night. . . .

Setting the big goals wasn't as hard as breaking them down: What rocks need to be moved to achieve them? That's one of the beauties of working with Bill and Melinda. They want to see progress, but bold goals don't faze them.

---

* As the Gates Foundation made a series of eight-figure grant awards to the Carter Center, the number of reported cases of Guinea worm disease dropped from 75,223 in 2000 to 4,619 in 2008 to just 22 in 2015. *Dracunculiasis*, its scientific name, is now expected to become the second disease in human history to be eradicated, after smallpox.

Case in point: the ongoing fight against the most lethal animal on the planet, the mosquito.* In 2016, the Gates Foundation teamed with the British government in a five-year, $4.3 billion campaign to eradicate malaria, the deadliest of all tropical diseases. Driven by empirical data, they have broadened their focus from a transmission-blocking vaccine to a comprehensive eradication strategy.

OBJECTIVE

Global eradication of malaria by 2040

KEY RESULTS

1. **Prove to the world that a radical cure-based approach can lead to regional elimination.**

2. **Prepare for scale-up by creating the necessary tools—SERCAP (Single Exposure Radical Cure and Prophylaxis) Diagnostic.**

3. **Sustain current global progress to ensure the environment is conducive to eradication push.**

The top-line objective is to eliminate the *Plasmodium* parasite from the human population, with a special emphasis on drug-resistant strains. As Bill Gates himself has acknowledged, this effort won't be easy. But it has a real chance to succeed because his team is tracking what matters.

---

* According to the World Health Organization, the mosquito is responsible for 725,000 deaths per year. Female *Anopheles* mosquitoes, the ones that transmit malaria, by themselves killed an estimated 429,000 people in 2015, with an upper range of 639,000. By way of comparison, human beings kill approximately 475,000 people per year, on average. No other species comes close.

12

Superpower #4:
Stretch for Amazing

The biggest risk of all is not taking one.

—*Mellody Hobson*

O KRs push us far beyond our comfort zones. They lead us to achievements on the border between abilities and dreams. They unearth fresh capacity, hatch more creative solutions, revolutionize business models. For companies seeking to live long and prosper, stretching to new heights is compulsory. As Bill Campbell liked to say: If companies "don't continue to innovate, they're going to die—and I didn't say *iterate*, I said *innovate*." Conservative goal setting stymies innovation. And innovation is like oxygen: You cannot win without it.

When stretch goals are chosen wisely, the payoff merits the risk and then some. "Big Hairy Audacious Goals"—Jim Collins's memorable phrase in *Good to Great*—spark leaps to new levels:

A BHAG is a huge and daunting goal—like a big mountain to climb. It is clear, compelling, and people "get it" right away. A BHAG serves as a unifying focal point of effort, galvanizing people and creating team spirit as people strive toward a finish line. Like the 1960s NASA moon mission, a BHAG captures the imagination and grabs people in the gut.

Edwin Locke, the patriarch of structured goal setting, mined a dozen studies for a quantitative correlation between goal difficulty and achievement. The arenas ranged widely, but the results were "unequivocal," Locke wrote. "[T]he harder the goal the higher the level of performance. . . . Although subjects with very hard goals reached their goals far less often than subjects with very easy goals, the former consistently performed at a higher level than the latter." The studies found that "stretched" workers were not only more productive, but more motivated and engaged: "Setting specific challenging goals is also a means of enhancing task interest and of helping people to discover the pleasurable aspects of an activity."

In 2007, the National Academy of Engineering asked a panel of leading thinkers—including Larry Page, futurist Ray Kurzweil, and geneticist J. Craig Venter—to choose fourteen "Grand Engineering Challenges" for the twenty-first century. After a year of debate, the panel settled on an array of quintessential stretch goals: Generate energy from fusion. Reverse-engineer the brain. Prevent nuclear terror. Secure cyberspace. (You get the picture.)

Not all stretch goals are so rarefied. Sometimes they represent "ordinary" work at an extraordinary level. But regardless of scope or scale, they fit my favorite definition of entrepreneurs:

*Those who do more than anyone thinks possible . . . with less than anyone thinks possible.**

At fledgling start-ups and market leaders alike, stretch goals

---

* By contrast with bureaucrats, who do less than anyone thinks possible with more than anyone thinks possible.

can sharpen an entrepreneurial culture. By pushing people past old limits, they are forces for operating excellence. As Philip Potloff, chief digital officer at Edmunds.com, noted, "We're trying to change the way automotive retailing is conducted, and that's a massive challenge and a massive opportunity. The only way for us to boil down our crazy, big, 'change-the industry' goals is through OKRs. It's why OKRs continue to be at the center of what we do."

Aspirational goals draw on every OKR superpower. *Focus* and *commitment* are a must for targeting goals that make a real difference. Only a transparent, collaborative, *aligned*, and *connected* organization can achieve so far beyond the norm. And without quantifiable *tracking*, how can you know when you've reached that amazing *stretch* objective?

Two OKR Baskets

Google divides its OKRs into two categories, committed goals and aspirational (or "stretch") goals. It's a distinction with a real difference.

Committed objectives are tied to Google's metrics: product releases, bookings, hiring, customers. Management sets them at the company level, employees at the departmental level. In general, these committed objectives—such as sales and revenue goals—are to be achieved in full (100 percent) within a set time frame.

Aspirational objectives reflect bigger-picture, higher-risk, more future-tilting ideas. They originate from any tier and aim to mobilize the entire organization. By definition, they are challenging to achieve. Failures—at an average rate of 40 percent—are part of Google's territory.

The relative weighting of these two baskets is a cultural question. It will vary from one organization to the next, and from quarter to quarter. Leaders must ask themselves: What type of company do we need to be in the coming year? Agile and daring, to crack a new market—or more conservative and operational, to firm up our existing position? Are we in survival mode, or is there cash on hand to bet big for a big reward? What does our business require, right now?

Our Need to Stretch

Andy Grove was a fan of Abraham Maslow, the mid-twentieth-century psychologist best known for his "hierarchy of needs." According to Maslow, only after we satisfy more basic concerns—starting with food and shelter, then safety, then "love" and "belongingness"—can we move to higher-level motivations. At the top of Maslow's pyramid stands the need for "self-actualization":

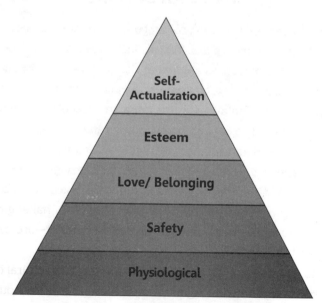

Maslow's hierarchy of needs represented as a pyramid, with more basic needs at the base.

Grove was fascinated to find that some people, with no prompting, were consistently driven to "try to test the outer limits of their abilities" and achieve their "personal best." These employees were a manager's dream; they were never self-satisfied. But Grove also understood that not everyone was a natural-born achiever. For the rest, "stretched" goals could elicit maximum output: "Such goal-setting is extremely important if you want peak performance from yourself and your subordinates."

Intel treasured calculated risk takers. It was the place I learned to stretch and to dare to fail. In Operation Crush, the do-or-die campaign to dominate the 16-bit chip microprocessor market, the company's salespeople were measured by design wins, the number of products designed around our 8086 microprocessor. Led by Bill Davidow, the Crush task force set one of the bolder goals I've ever seen: one thousand design wins in a single calendar year, 50 percent more than sales had logged the year before. Here is what happened next, as recalled by Dave House, general manager for microprocessors:

> This is Intel; you've got to measure it. And I think it was [Jim] Lally who said, we need 1,000 design wins. It was a number; it was either Bill or Jim. . . . And it seemed like an enormous number. And then as we were developing our plans, somehow that number got changed to 2,000. And that wound up being the number we would take to field sales.

Two thousand design wins equated to one win per salesperson per month. Management was asking our field reps to *triple* their numbers for a chip so unpopular that longtime customers were hanging up on them. The sales force was beaten down and defeated, and now it stared up at Mount Everest. When I recently asked Bill Davidow about setting such a steep objective, he replied, "I picked the two thousand because I thought we needed a rallying point. And that was a rallying point."

The company incentivized the reps with a trip for two to Tahiti for all who reached the mark. Then Jim Lally added an ingenious stipulation: If a single individual failed to make the quota, the straggler's entire district office would lose out on the trip. Early on, the numbers badly trailed the target, until the task force began to think about relaxing the design win criterion. But that summer, full-color Tahiti brochures mysteriously found their way into every salesperson's home mailbox. By the third quarter, peer pressure on the laggards was enormous.

At year's end, the design win tally exceeded 2,300. The 8086 reigned supreme in the marketplace; Intel's future was assured. Virtually the entire sales force went to Tahiti. And a stretch goal had made all the difference.

The Gospel of 10x

If Andy Grove is the patron saint of aspirational OKRs, Larry Page is their latter-day high priest. In technology, Google stands for boundless innovation and relentless growth. In the world of objectives and key results, the company is synonymous with exponentially aggressive goals, or what author Steven Levy calls "the gospel of 10x."

Consider Gmail. The main problem with earlier web-based email systems was meager storage, typically 2 to 4 megabytes. Users were forced to delete old emails to make room for new ones. Archives were a pipe dream. During Gmail's development, Google's leaders considered offering 100MB of storage—an enormous upgrade. But by 2004, when the product was released to the public, the 100MB goal was dead and forgotten. Instead, Gmail provided a full *gigabyte* of storage, up to five hundred times more than the competition. Users could keep emails in perpetuity. Digital communication changed forever.

That, my friends, is a Big Hairy Audacious Goal. Gmail didn't merely improve on existing systems. It reinvented the category and forced competitors to raise their game by orders of magnitude. Such 10x thinking is rare in any sector, on any stage. Most people, Larry Page observes, "tend to assume that things are impossible, rather than starting from real-world physics and figuring out what's actually possible."

In *Wired*, Steven Levy elaborated:

> The way Page sees it, a ten percent improvement means that you're doing the same thing as everybody else. You probably won't fail spectacularly, but you are guaranteed not to succeed wildly.
>
> That's why Page expects Googlers to create products and services that are ten times better than the competition. That means he isn't satisfied with discovering a couple of hidden efficiencies or tweaking code to achieve modest gains. Thousand percent improvement requires rethinking problems, exploring what's technically possible and having fun in the process.

At Google, in line with Andy Grove's old standard, aspirational OKRs are set at 60 to 70 percent attainment. In other words, performance is expected to fall short at least 30 percent of the time. And that's considered success!

Eric Schmidt, Larry Page, and Sergey Brin with Google's
first self-driving car, 2011—10x thinking in action!

Google has had its share of colossal misfires, from Helpouts to Google Answers. Living in the 70 percent zone entails a liberal sprinkling of moonshots and a willingness to court failure. At the start of the period, not a single goal may look possible. And so the Googlers are pushed to ask harder questions: What radical, high-risk action needs to be considered? What do they need to *stop* doing? Where can they move resources or find new partners? By deadline, a healthy fraction of those impossible goals are somehow attained in full.

Stretch Variables

To succeed, a stretch goal cannot seem like a long march to nowhere. Nor can it be imposed from on high without regard to realities on the ground. Stretch your team too fast and too far, and it may snap. In pursuing high-effort, high-risk goals, employee commitment is essential. Leaders must convey two things: the importance of the outcome, and the belief that it's attainable.

Few entities have Google's resources to fall back upon when a moonshot crashes. Organizations have a range of risk tolerance, which may change over time. The greater the margin for error, the more a company can extend itself. For example, a 40 percent OKR failure rate might seem too risky—and too discouraging, no matter what leadership says. For high achievers, anything shy of perfection can sap morale. At Risk Management Solutions in California, there are "more degrees than employees," says Amelia Merrill, a former HR leader. "People here are used to getting A's. They don't get B's. Not getting 100 percent—that's just really hard, culturally, to make that transition."

At MyFitnessPal, Mike Lee considers *all* OKRs to be committed goals: difficult and demanding, yes, but attainable in full. "I am trying to set the bar right at where I think it should be," he says. "If we get them all done, I'll feel good about our progress." That's a reasonable approach, but not without pitfalls. Will Mike's people shy away from objectives where they might top out at 90 percent? In my view, it's better for leaders to set at least a modest stretch. Over time, as teams and individuals gain experience with OKRs, their key results will become more precise *and* more aggressive.

There is no one magic number for the "right" stretch. But consider this: How can your team create maximum value? What would *amazing* look like? If you seek to achieve greatness, stretching for amazing is a great place to start. But by no means, as Andy Grove made clear, is it the place to stop:

> You know, in our business we have to set ourselves uncomfortably tough objectives, and then we have to meet them. *And then after ten milliseconds of celebration* we have to set ourselves another [set of] highly difficult-to-reach objectives and we have to meet them. And the reward of having met one of these challenging goals is that you get to play again.

13

Stretch:
The Google Chrome Story

Sundar Pichai
CEO

Stretch goals were beautifully defined by the leader of the Google X team that developed Project Loon and self-driving cars. Says Astro Teller: "If you want your car to get fifty miles per gallon, fine. You can retool your car a little bit. But if I tell you it has to run on a gallon of gas for five hundred miles, you have to start over."

In 2008, Sundar Pichai was Google's vice president of product development. When Sundar and his team took their Chrome browser to market, they were most definitely starting over. Driven to succeed but unafraid of failure, they used OKRs to catapult their product—and their company—to amazing. Chrome is now the most popular web browser by far on both the mobile and desktop platforms. As you will see, there were bumps in the road. But as Larry Page says, "If you set a crazy, ambitious goal and miss it, you'll still achieve something remarkable." When you aim for the stars, you may come up short but still reach the moon.

The career of Sundar Pichai is a stretch goal personified. In

October 2015, at age forty-three, Sundar became Google's third CEO. Today he presides over an organization with more than sixty thousand employees and $80 billion in revenues.

————

Sundar Pichai: Growing up in South India in the 1980s, I had scant exposure to technology as we see it today. Yet what we had made a profound impact on my life. My father was an electrical engineer in Chennai, a great metropolis, but we lived modestly. The waiting list for a telephone—a rotary dial model—was three to four years. I was twelve years old when my family finally got one. It was a big event. Neighbors would come and use it.

I remember my life as pre-phone and post-phone; that one device changed so many things. Pre-phone, my mother would say, "Can you see if the blood test is ready in the hospital?" I would catch a bus and ride to the hospital, and wait in line, and often they would tell me, "No, it isn't ready yet, come tomorrow." By the time I rode the bus home, it was a three-hour trip. Post-phone, I could simply call the hospital and know the results. Now we take technology for granted, and it gets better every day. But for me there were these discrete moments, before and after, that I will never forget.

I read every book about computers and semiconductors that I could lay my hands on. I aspired to somehow make it to Silicon Valley, which meant getting into Stanford—that was my goal, to be a part of all the change happening there. In a way, I think I dreamt even more fervently because so little technology was available to us. I was driven by the power of imagining.

The New Applications Platform

For five years, I worked at Applied Materials in Santa Clara, in process engineering, R&D. Sometimes I would need to go to Intel, and I could feel the Andy Grove culture as soon as I stepped inside the door. The company was very disciplined, down to the smallest thing. (I vaguely remember having paid for each cup of coffee.) In semiconductor process engineering, you must be highly methodical in setting your goals and working your way through them. So my work at Applied Materials helped me think about goals in a more precise way.

As the internet continued to develop, I could see its tremendous potential. I read about everything Google was doing—I was passionate on the subject. I was especially excited when they launched a product called Deskbar, where you could search the web from Windows without opening the browser—it launched from a small window in the taskbar. It was there when you needed it, but only then. Deskbar was an early tool for growth, a way to bring Google to many more people.

I joined Google as a product manager in 2004, when the company still revolved around search. But that was also the year of Web 2.0 and the rise of user-generated content and AJAX.* The early web was a content platform, but it was fast becoming an applications platform. We were seeing the beginning of a paradigm shift on the internet, and I sensed that Google would be at the heart of it.

My first assignment was to expand the use and distribution of Google Toolbar, which could be added to any browser to get you to Google Search. It was the right project for the right time. In just a

---

* A module of web-development techniques that enabled users to communicate with a server without reloading a page or refreshing the browser.

few years, we scaled up Toolbar users by more than 10x. That was when I first saw the power of an ambitious, stretch OKR.

Rethinking the Browser

By then we'd set up something new for Google, a team to build client software. We had people working on Firefox to help improve Mozilla's browser. By 2006, we were beginning to rethink the browser as a computing platform, almost like an operating system, so that people could write applications on the web itself. That fundamental insight gave birth to Chrome. We knew we needed a multiprocess architecture to make each tab its own process and protect a user's Gmail if another application crashed. And we knew we had to get JavaScript working a lot faster. But we were up for the task of building the best browser possible.

Eric Schmidt, our CEO, knew how hard it was to construct a browser from scratch: "If you're doing it, you had better be serious about it." If Chrome wasn't going to be dramatically different and better and faster than the traditional browsers already on the market, there was no point in moving ahead.

In 2008, the year of Chrome's rollout, our product management team formulated a top-level annual objective that would have an enduring influence on Google's future: to "develop the next-generation client platform for web applications." The main key result: "Chrome reaches 20 million seven-day active users."

Upping the Goal

In Google's OKR climate, it was understood that 70 percent achievement (on average) was considered a success. You weren't supposed to strive for greens on every OKR you wrote—that wouldn't stretch the team. But there was an intrinsic tension because you didn't get hired at Google unless you were driven to succeed. As a leader, you didn't want to find yourself at the end of the quarter, standing in front of the company with a big red on the screen, having to explain why and how you failed. The pressure and discomfort of that experience made a lot of us do a lot of heroic things to avoid it. But if you set your team's objectives correctly, it was sometimes unavoidable.

Larry was always good about upping the goals for the company OKRs. He used certain phrases that stuck with me. He wanted people at Google to be "uncomfortably excited." He wanted us to have "a healthy disregard for the impossible." I tried to do the same for the products team. It took courage to write an OKR that might well fail, but there was no other way if we wanted to be great. We deliberately set the bar for 20 million weekly active users by year's end, knowing it was a formidable stretch—we were starting from zero, after all.

As a leader, you must try to challenge the team without making them feel the goal is unachievable. I thought it unlikely we would reach our target in time. (Candidly, I thought there was no way we would get there.) But I also considered it important to keep pushing to the limit of our ability and beyond. By putting the 20 million out there, I knew good things would happen. Our stretch OKR gave the team direction and a barometer to measure our progress. It made complacency impossible. And it kept us all rethinking, every day, the framework for what we were doing. All of these things were more important than reaching a somewhat arbitrary target on a designated day.

Early on, as Chrome struggled to reach 3 percent market share, we received some unanticipated bad news. The Mac version of Chrome fell way behind schedule. Only Windows users would count toward the 20 million.

But there was good news, too—people who used Chrome loved it, which was starting to have a compounding effect on growth. Glitches notwithstanding, we were driving awareness of a new way to engage the web. We just needed to find more users, and sooner than later.

Digging Deeper

Google stands for speed. The company has waged a constant battle against latency, the delay in a data transfer that degrades the user experience. In 2008, Larry and Sergey wrote a beautiful OKR that truly captured people's attention: "We should make the web as fast as flipping through a magazine." It inspired the whole company to think harder about how we could make things better and faster.

For the Chrome project, we created a sub-OKR to turbocharge JavaScript. The goal was to make applications on the web work as smoothly as downloads on a desktop. We set a moonshot goal of 10x improvement and named the project "V8," after the high-performance car engine. We were fortunate to find a Danish programmer named Lars Bak, who'd built virtual machines for Sun Microsystems and held more than a dozen patents. Lars is one of the great artists in his field. He came to us and said, without an ounce of bravado, "I can do something that is much, much faster." Within four months, he had JavaScript running ten times as fast as it ran on Firefox. Within two years, it was more than twenty times faster—incredible progress. (Sometimes a stretch goal is not as wildly aspirational as it may seem. As Lars later told Steven Levy in *In the Plex*, "We sort of underestimated what we could do.")

Stretch OKRs are an intense exercise in problem solving. Having gone through the Toolbar journey, I had a good sense of how to work my way through the inevitable troughs. Sure, there were sleepless nights. But no matter how much stress I was feeling, I stayed cautiously optimistic with my team. If we were losing users, I would tell them, let's do an experiment to understand why and fix it. If compatibility was an issue, I'd assign a group to focus on that. I tried to be thoughtful and systematic and not too emotional, and I think that helped.

Google is propelled by our moonshot culture. The very ambitious is very hard to do. In a healthy way, our team realized that the success of Chrome would ultimately mean hundreds of millions of users. Whenever we invent something new at Google, we're always thinking: How can we scale it to a billion? Early in the process, that number can seem very abstract. But when you set a measurable objective for the year and chunk the problem, quarter by quarter, moonshots become more doable. That's one of the great benefits of OKRs. They give us clear, quantitative targets on the road to those qualitative leaps.

After we failed against the 20 million in 2008, it made us dig deeper. We never gave up on the objective, but we changed the way we framed it. Here's what I tried to communicate: "No, we didn't reach the goal, but we are laying the foundation to break through this barrier. Now, what are we going to do differently?" In a culture of smart people, you had better have good answers to that question; you can't tap-dance your way through. In this case, we needed a solution to one very basic problem: Why was it so difficult to get people to try a new browser?

That's how we became motivated to find new distribution deals for Chrome. Down the road, when we found that people were unclear about just what a browser did for them, we turned to television marketing to explain it. Our Chrome ads represented the largest offline campaign in the company's history. People still remember "Dear Sophie,"* a spot created around a father's digital scrapbook of his daughter as she grew. It showed the easy entrée from our browser to such a rich stock of web-based applications, from Gmail and YouTube to Google Maps. It led people to the internet as an applications platform.

Try-Fail, Try-Succeed

Success was not instantaneous. In 2009, we set another stretch OKR for Chrome—50 million seven-day active users—and failed again, ending the year at 38 million. For 2010, undeterred, I proposed a target of 100 million users. Larry believed we should be pushing even harder. My target, he pointed out, touched only 10 percent of the world's one billion internet users at the time. I countered that 100 million was in fact very aggressive.

Larry and I eventually settled on an OKR of 111 million users, a classic stretch goal. To reach it, we knew we'd need to reinvent the business of Chrome and think about growth in new ways. Again, what could we do differently? In February, we broadened our distribution deals with the OEMs [original equipment manufacturers]. In March, we embarked on a "Chrome Fast" marketing campaign to heighten product awareness in the United States. In May, we expanded our demographic by launching Chrome for OS X and Linux. At last, our browser was no longer a Windows-only product.

* www.whatmatters.com/dearsophie.

Well into the third quarter, the outcome remained in doubt. Then we did a small thing that became a big thing: a passive alert for former Chrome users who'd been dormant. Weeks later, at the end of Q3, our user total had surged from 87 million to 107 million. And shortly after that, we reached 111 million seven-day actives. We had achieved our goal.

Today, on mobile alone, there are more than a billion active users of Chrome. We couldn't have gotten there without objectives and key results. OKRs are the way we think about everything at Google, the way we've always done it.

Sundar presents his Chrome keynote at Google's I/O developer conference, 2013.

The Next Frontier

My father came of age in a time when computing meant huge teams and mainframes and system administrators—when computers were both inaccessible and very complicated. By the time I was working on Chrome, I realized that all he wanted was an easy, straightforward way to use the web. I've always been fascinated by simplicity. For all the complex things Google Search could do, the user experience was phenomenally uncomplicated. I wanted to emulate that quality in our browser—to the point where you could be a kid in India or a professor at Stanford, and it wouldn't matter. If you had access to a computer and adequate connectivity, your experience with Chrome would be manifestly simple.*

In 2008, when my father was retired, I gave him a netbook and showed him how to use Chrome. And then an amazing thing happened for him: The technology just faded away. He could just do whatever he wanted on the thriving applications platform on the web. Once he got into our browser, he never opened another app. He never downloaded another piece of software. He lived in Chrome. He surrendered into a new and wonderfully simple world.

At Google, from very early on, I internalized the need to constantly imagine the next frontier—from Toolbar to Chrome, for example. You can never stop stretching. My father's experience got us thinking: What if we could design an operating system with comparable simplicity and security, with the Chrome browser as its user

---

* I had the great good fortune of working on Chrome and even sharing an office with Linus Upson, who led the team's engineering group. At the end of the workday I could never tell whether Linus had left or not because his desk was always so clean. (If one of his pens was lying at an angle, I knew something was wrong.) Linus had a maniacal focus on simplicity. He gave us the cutting edge we needed to make Chrome the seamless experience it is today.

interface? And what if we could invent a laptop around that operating system—a Chromebook—to tap directly into all of those applications living in the cloud?

But those would be stretch goals for another day.

14

Stretch:
The YouTube Story

Susan Wojcicki
CEO

Cristos Goodrow
Vice President of Engineering

Google is so teeming with stretch goals that it would feel incomplete to chronicle only one of them. And so here is a second, the story of YouTube and how it grew— exponentially—with the "stretch" OKR superpower.

Susan Wojcicki, according to *Time* magazine, is "the most powerful woman on the internet." She's played a central role at Google from the start, even before becoming employee No. 16 and the company's first marketing manager. In September 1998, days after Google was incorporated, Susan rented out her Menlo Park garage for the company's first office. Eight years later, as analysts doubted that YouTube would survive, she was a leading voice in persuading Google's board to acquire it. Susan had the vision to see that online video was about to disrupt network television— forever.

Susan Wojcicki and her Menlo Park garage, where it all began.

By 2012, YouTube had become a market leader and one of the biggest video platforms in the world. But its furious pace of innovation had slowed—and once you brake, it's not easy to reaccelerate. By that point, Susan had risen to senior vice president of advertising and commerce, where she reimagined AdWords and envisioned a new way to monetize the web with AdSense. (Basically, she drove the success of Google's two main revenue streams.) In 2014, as the new CEO of YouTube, she inherited one of the most aggressive goals anytime, anywhere. Over a span of four years, the mission was to reach a billion hours of people watching YouTube every day—to grow by a factor of ten. But Susan didn't want to grow at any cost—she wanted to do this responsibly. Susan and a veteran YouTube engineering leader, Cristos Goodrow, had their work cut out for them. They would rely on OKRs every step of the way.

Stretch goals are invigorating. By committing to radical, qualitative improvement, an established organization can renew its sense of urgency and reap tremendous dividends. YouTube's once struggling web video business has scaled to more than a billion users, nearly a third of the total population on the internet. Its site can be navigated in more than seventy different languages in more than eighty countries. Its mobile platform alone reaches more eighteen-to-forty-nine-year-olds than any cable or broadcast network.

None of this happened by accident, or by the grace of a single insight. It took years of rigorous execution, meticulous attention to detail, and the structure and discipline of OKRs. And one more thing: Before YouTube could begin to chase its monumentally audacious objective, first it had to figure out how to measure what mattered.

———

Susan Wojcicki: When I leased my garage to Larry and Sergey, I had no interest in Google as a company. I just wanted them to pay the rent. But then I got to know them and how they thought about things. I had ideas for starting my own company, but it dawned on me that Larry and Sergey were better positioned to execute them. And then there was the day Google Search went down and I couldn't get my work done. Google, I realized, had become an indispensable tool; I couldn't live without it. And I thought, *This is going to be important for everyone.*

I was there when John Doerr came to talk to us about OKRs in the fall of 1999. By then we'd outgrown my garage and moved to 2400 Bayshore in Mountain View, an old Sun Microsystems plant. The whole building might have been 42,000 square feet, and we operated in less than half of it. We had the OKR meeting in the other half, the part reserved for all-hands. I can remember John explaining the concept: "This is an objective. This is a key result." And using the football analogy to demonstrate how OKRs were implemented. The other day, sorting through some files, I came across John's presentation—on plastic laminate sheets for an overhead projector. That's how old it was.

Larry and Sergey were good at listening to people who knew what they were talking about. I'm sure they argued with John, but they listened. They had never run a company or even worked in a company before. John came in and said, "This is a way you can run your business, and it's measurable and trackable." Measurables were intuitive to Larry and Sergey, and they had to be impressed by the fact that Intel used OKRs. Intel was such a great company, and we were so small by comparison.

Judging from our experience at Google, I'd say that OKRs are especially useful for young companies just starting to build their culture. When you're little, with fewer resources, it's even more vital to be clear on where you're going. It's like raising kids. If you bring them up with no structure, and then you tell them as teenagers, "Okay, now here are the rules"—well, that's going to be hard. If possible, it's better to have rules from the start. At the same time, I've seen mature companies do turnarounds and change people and processes. No company is too young to adopt OKRs, and for no company is it too late.

OKRs require organization. You need a leader to embrace the process and a lieutenant to ride herd over scoring and reviews. When I ran OKRs for Larry, I sat in on four-hour meetings with his leadership team, where he'd debate all the company objectives and people were expected to be able to defend them and make sure they were clear. The guidance for OKRs at Google was often top-down, but with lots of discussion with experts on the team and significant give-and-take on key results: *This is the direction we want to go, now tell us how you're going to get there.* Those long meetings enabled Larry to emphasize things he cared about, and also to vent frustrations, especially around service on our product OKRs. He'd say, "Tell me your speed now." And then: "Why can't you cut that in half?"

We still conduct our all-hands, top-level OKR meeting in a special videocast each quarter, though Google is now so large and multifaceted that it's hard to communicate everything we do to everyone. At one memorable all-hands, Salar Kamangar, my predecessor as YouTube CEO, did an amazing job running through the company's entire OKR roster. (Salar can put anything into context.) But in general, the more detailed discussions take place within our teams. And you'll still find OKRs posted on the company and team pages on Google's intranet, updated in real time, where any contributor can access and review them.

If You Can't Beat 'Em . . .

Google Videos, our free video-sharing website, launched in 2005, one month before YouTube. When I ran it, the first clip we uploaded for users was a purple Muppet singing a nonsense song from an Italian movie about sex in Sweden. Sergey and I weren't sure what to make of it. But then my kids shouted, "Play it again!" The light bulb went on. We saw a next-generation opportunity, a new way for people to create video for global distribution. We went about building an interface, and had our surprising first hit: two kids singing Backstreet Boys in their dorm room, with a roommate studying in the background. We carried some professional videos, too, but the user-generated content did better.

The main flaw in Google Videos was a delay in our upload process. It broke a company rule for product development: Make it fast. User-uploaded videos weren't immediately available to watch, whereas on YouTube they were—a big problem. By the time we fixed it, we'd lost significant market share. YouTube was out-streaming us three to one, but financially they were struggling. Swamped by demand, they urgently needed capital to build infrastructure. It was clear they would have to sell.

I saw an opportunity to combine the two services. I worked up some spreadsheets to justify the $1.65 billion purchase price, to show that Google could make its money back, and convinced Larry and Sergey. At the last minute, the founders asked me to bring my spreadsheets to the board meeting. There were lots of questions. The board gave us the green light, though they weren't totally sold on my assumption for year-on-year user growth. And it's funny, because rapid growth is the one thing that YouTube has consistently delivered to this day.

Big Rocks

Cristos Goodrow: In February 2011, when I came over from Google Product Search, three years before Susan joined the team, YouTube's OKRs needed work. The company—around eight hundred people at the time—was producing hundreds of them each quarter. A team would open a Google doc and start typing in objectives, and they'd wind up with thirty or forty for ten people, and less than half would actually get done.

Engineers struggle with goal setting in two big ways. They hate crossing off anything they think is a good idea, and they habitually underestimate how long it takes to get things done. I'd lived through this at Product Search, where they'd insist: "Come on, I'm a smart person. I can surely get more done than *that*." It took discipline for people to narrow their lists to three or four objectives for their team, but it made a huge difference. Our OKRs became more rigorous. Everybody knew what counted most. After I took responsibility for search and discovery at YouTube, it only made sense to do the same thing there.

Then Salar Kamangar turned over day-to-day leadership for the tech side of YouTube to Shishir Mehrotra, and Shishir helped bring focus to the whole company. He used a metaphor called the Big Rocks Theory, which was popularized by Stephen Covey. Say you have some rocks, and a bunch of pebbles, and some sand, and your goal is to fit as much of everything as you can into a wide-mouth, one-gallon jar. If you start with the sand, and then the pebbles, the jar will run out of room for all the rocks. But when you start with the rocks, add the pebbles, and save the sand for last, the sand fills the spaces between the rocks—everything fits. In other words, the most important things need to get done first or they won't get done at all.

But what were YouTube's big rocks? People did their own things and let a thousand flowers bloom, but no one could identify the top-level OKRs. Now leadership was saying, "All of your ideas are wonderful. But could we please identify a few of them as our big rocks for this quarter, and for the year?" After that, everyone at YouTube knew our top priorities. All of our big rocks would make it into the jar.

That was a giant step toward the goal that swallowed the next four years of my life.

A Better Metric

YouTube had figured out how to make money, but they still weren't sure how to grow viewership. Fortunately for the company and me, an engineer in Google Research Group was out in front of us. On a dedicated team named Sibyl, Jim McFadden was building a system for selecting "watch next" recommendations, aka related videos or "suggestions." It had tremendous potential to boost our overall views. But were views what we really wanted to boost?

As Microsoft CEO Satya Nadella has pointed out: In a world where computing power is nearly limitless, "the true scarce commodity is increasingly human attention." When users spend more of their valuable time watching YouTube videos, they must perforce be happier with those videos. It's a virtuous circle: More satisfied viewership (watch time) begets more advertising, which incentivizes more content creators, which draws more viewership.

Our true currency wasn't views or clicks—it was watch time. The logic was undeniable. YouTube needed a new core metric.

Watch Time, and Only Watch Time

In September 2011, I sent a provocative email to my boss and the YouTube leadership team. Subject line: "Watch time, and only watch time." It was a call to rethink how we measured success: "All other things being equal, our goal is to increase [video] watch time." For many folks at Google, it smacked of heresy. Google Search was designed as a switchboard to route you off the site and out to your best destination as quickly as possible. Maximizing watch time was antithetical to its purpose in life. Moreover, watch time would be negative for views, the critical metric for both users and creators. Last (but not least), to optimize for watch time would incur a significant money hit, at least at the start. Since YouTube ads were shown exclusively before videos started, fewer starts meant fewer ads. Fewer ads meant less revenue.*

My argument was that Google and YouTube were different animals. To make the dichotomy as stark as possible, I made up a scenario: A user goes to YouTube and types the query "How do I tie a bow tie?" And we have two videos on the topic. The first is one minute long and teaches you very quickly and precisely how to tie a bow tie. The second is ten minutes long and is full of jokes and really entertaining, and at the end of it you may or may not know how to tie a bow tie. I'd ask my colleagues: Which video should be ranked as our first search result?

For those at Google Search, the answer was easy: "The first one, of course. If people come to YouTube to tie a bow tie, we surely want to help them tie a bow tie."

And I'd say, "I want to show them the second video."

And the Search cohort would protest, "Why would you do that? These poor people just want to tie their bow ties and get to their event!" (They were probably thinking: This guy's insane.) But my point was that YouTube's mission was fundamentally divergent. It's fine for viewers to learn to tie bow ties, and if that's *all* they want, they'll choose the one-minute manual. But that's not what YouTube was about, not really. Our job was to keep people engaged and hanging out with us. By definition, viewers are happier watching seven minutes of a ten-minute video (or even two minutes of a ten-minute video) than *all* of a one-minute video. And when they're happier, we are, too.

---

* Though it's a work in progress, YouTube now intersperses some ads mid-video, to correspond to its new definition of value.

It took six months, but I won the argument. On the Ides of March, 2012, we launched a watch-time-optimized version of our recommendation algorithm aimed at improving user engagement and satisfaction.

A Big Round Number

In November 2012, at our annual YouTube Leadership Summit in Los Angeles, Shishir gathered a few of us together. He said he was about to announce a big stretch goal to kick off the coming year: one billion hours in daily user watch time. (There is power in simplicity, and round numbers are simple.) He asked us, "When can we get this done? What's the time frame?" A billion hours represented a 10x increase, and we knew it would take years, not months. We thought 2015 was too soon, and 2017 sounded weird. (Prime numbers, in general, sound weird.) Just before Shishir took the stage, we settled on the end of 2016, a four-year OKR with a set of rolling, annual objectives and quarterly, incremental key results.

> **OBJECTIVE**
> Reach 1 billion hours of watch time per day [by 2016], with growth driven by:
>
> **KEY RESULTS**
> 1. Search team + Main App (+XX%), Living Room (+XX%).
> 2. Grow kids' engagement and gaming watch time (X watch hours per day).
> 3. Launch YouTube VR experience and grow VR catalog from X to Y videos.

Principled Stretching

Stretch goals can be crushing if people don't believe they're achievable. That's where the art of framing comes in. Clever manager that he is, Shishir cut our BHAG down to size. While one billion daily hours sounded like an awful lot, it represented less than 20 percent of the world's total television watch time. Introducing that context was helpful and clarifying, at least for me. We weren't gunning to be arbitrarily big. Rather: There was another thing out there way bigger than us, and we were trying to scale up to it.

In pursuing our mission over the next four years, we weren't 10x absolutists. In fact, we'd commit to some watch-time-negative decisions for the benefit of our users. For example, we made it a policy to stop recommending trashy, tabloid-style videos—like "World's Worst Parents," where the thumbnail showed a baby in a pot on the stove. Three weeks in, the move proved negative for watch time by half a percent. We stood by our decision because it was better for the viewer experience, cut down on click bait, and reflected our principle of growing responsibly. Three months in, watch time in this group had bounced back and actually *increased*. Once the gruesome stuff became less accessible, people sought out more satisfying content.

Once the billion-hour BHAG was set, however, we never did *anything* without measuring impact on watch time. If a change might slow our progress, we'd be scrupulous about estimating just how much. Then we'd build internal consensus before going through with it.

Getting Up to Speed

Susan: Salar Kamangar most enjoys the earlier stages of companies. He likes taking them to the next level; he's really good at that. By 2012, YouTube had grown into a big organization, and Salar decided to move on. The company had split into two factions, business and technology, and needed someone to bring them together. After leading AdWords for a decade, I was used to complex ecosystems. I was eager to take on the challenge of unifying YouTube.

When YouTube leadership set the one-billion-hour daily watch time goal, most of our people judged it impossible. They thought it would break the internet! But it seemed to me that such a clear and measurable objective would energize people, and I cheered them on.

By February 2014, when I came over, YouTube was nearly a third of the way through the four-year, mega-stretch OKR. But while the objective was well planted, it wasn't quite on pace. Watch-time growth had dropped significantly below what we needed to make our deadline, a source of stress for all involved. While Google aims for a grade of 0.7 (or 70 percent attainment) on stretch goals in aggregate, and there are times people totally fail, no team goes into an OKR saying, "Let's settle for 70 percent and call it a success." Everyone tries to get to 100 percent, especially once an objective seems within reach. It's safe to say that no one at YouTube would have been satisfied to reach 700 million daily watch-time hours.

In all honesty, though, I wasn't certain we'd reach the billion hours on time. I thought it would be okay if we missed by a little bit, as long as everyone stayed united and aligned. I'd seen us miss objectives at Google, and we'd renew our focus and roll them forward. In 2007, when we introduced AdSense to monetize the whole web, the launch was a quarterly OKR. We worked really hard to release it to the actual day but wound up two days late. No harm was done.

Maybe the best thing about OKRs is how they track your progress to a target, especially when you're behind schedule. When I ran Google's mid-quarter OKR updates, the point was to figure out how to fix things and get back on track. The updates were opportunities to gather the leadership team and say, "Okay, I want each of you to name five projects you can implement to bring us closer to our goal." We'd extend the OKR and promote positive behavior. So I wasn't super-worried about hitting the billion hours before the clock struck twelve.

Cristos Goodrow, the OKR's guardian, had another perspective. The billion daily hours had become his white whale. Not long after I joined the company, at our "up-to-speed" meeting, Cristos presented me with a deck of forty-six slides. By number five, he'd made his point loud and clear: We needed to catch up.

Cristos: I was very concerned. Each year we announced our annual objectives and areas of focus. From 2013 through 2016, the billion-hour OKR headlined the presentation. We also had clear interim milestones to stay on track. When I first met with Susan, I thanked her for keeping our 10x goal. Then I said, "By the way, we're way behind. I'm freaked out and I hope that you're at least a little freaked out. And when you're making decisions about what to prioritize and where to lean, please keep in mind that we are not going to meet this watch-time OKR if we don't do something about it."

Susan: I had some pressing concerns. One was a rearguard action with Google's machine people, to make sure we had the infrastructure to support our goal. It takes a flood of bytes to get YouTube videos from our data centers to the user, way more than what's required for email or social media. (The technical term is "egress bandwidth.") We do everything we can to guarantee in advance that Google will have enough servers to route all those bytes to deliver your cat video to your phone or laptop.

After announcing the billion-hour OKR, YouTube's leadership team went on a charm offensive to reserve the bandwidth we'd need through 2016. When I took the reins, Google's server group asked to renegotiate what must have seemed like an exorbitant spend. I was in a tough spot: I was new, and we were lagging our projected usage. But if we cut back on our machines, I knew it wouldn't be easy to recover. So I kicked the can down the road. I said to those high-powered technical people, "Let's just stay with the plan for now and meet again in three months." I wanted to hang on to our reservations until we knew where things stood. Three months later, we had more data and more growth and an easier case to make.

The billion-hour OKR was a religion at YouTube, to the exclusion of nearly all else. It's important to respect people's religion, and I wanted to support that big stretch goal. But it was so black-and-white that I feared it could be detrimental if not properly managed. My job was to keep an eye on the gray, the nuances that might get overlooked. Daily watch time is driven by two factors: the average number of daily active viewers (or DAVs) and the average amount of time those viewers spend watching. YouTube was doing a good job on the second variable—but that was lower-hanging fruit. It's easier to expand a relationship than to get a new one started. Our research showed a lot more growth potential in enlarging our user base than in getting teenage boys to watch twice as much YouTube. We wanted new users—and so did our advertisers.

Mutual Support

Cristos: Whenever you get new leadership, everything's up for review. When Susan took over YouTube, she wasn't obligated to get behind the billion-hour OKR. That was the previous administration's goal. She could have reverted to a views goal, or one more oriented toward revenue. Or she could have kept the watch-time OKR but added three others of equal or greater priority. Had she done any of those things, we would never have reached the billion hours on time. We'd have gotten distracted and never caught up.

After Susan arrived, we began putting people's names next to our YouTube company goals, with colored bars denoting progress: green, yellow, or red. "Cristos" was listed cheek by jowl with "one billion hours" at every weekly staff meeting—quarter after quarter, year after year. I felt personally responsible for that OKR.

I appreciated the Google creed of setting risky, aggressive goals, and making it okay to fail against them. And I knew some good things had already happened. Since declaring the BHAG, my team had significantly improved video search and recommendations. We were the tip of an OKR spear that had raised YouTube's profile and stature throughout Google. The company's morale had never been higher. I'd hear marketing people discussing watch time with real fervor, something I never would have expected.

Even so, this OKR was different, for the company and for me. Early on I told Shishir that if we failed to make our four-year deadline, I'd resign from Google—and I meant it. I know that sounds melodramatic, but it's how I felt. And maybe that intensity of commitment helped me stick with it.

———

By New Year's 2016, the beginning of our gun lap, we were on schedule, but just barely. Then the warm-weather doldrums kicked in, with people spending more time outside and watching fewer videos. Would they ever come back? As late as July, our growth rate was lagging our year's-end goal. I was nervous enough to ask my team to think about reordering their projects to reaccelerate watch time.

In September, folks returned from their summer travels. As old viewers resumed their habits and new ones tuned in, all of our search and recommendations improvements were amplified. Reaching one billion hours was a game of inches; our engineers were hunting for changes that might yield as little as 0.2 percent more watch time. In 2016 alone, they would find around 150 of those tiny advances. We'd need nearly all of them to reach our objective.

By early October, daily watch time was growing well beyond our target rate. That's when I knew we were going to make it. Still, I kept checking our watch time graph every day, seven days a week. When I was on vacation. When I was sick. And then, one glorious Monday that fall, I checked again—and saw that we'd hit a billion hours over the weekend. We'd achieved the stretch OKR many thought was impossible, ahead of schedule.

The next day, for the first time in more than three years, I did not check the graph.

———

Our landmark OKR had some unanticipated consequences. Through the four-year push to reach the billion hours of daily watch time, our daily views soared in parallel. Stretch OKRs tend to set powerful forces into motion, and you can never be sure where they'll lead. Another big lesson, for me, was the importance of support from the top—from Susan, of course, but also from Larry and Sergey.

The founders weren't personally enmeshed in YouTube's business. They had no way to be certain we had chosen the best possible course, though I think they were happy it was ambitious and clear. But when lots of people in Google Search were openly skeptical about our OKR, both Larry and Sergey were willing to say onstage, "YouTube has this billion-hour goal, and they're still working toward it, and I support that." They gave us the autonomy we needed to meet the objective we'd set.

Susan Wojcicki celebrating YouTube's tenth birthday, 2015.

Thinking Bigger

Susan: Aspirational goals can prompt a reset for the entire organization. In our case, it inspired infrastructure initiatives throughout YouTube. People started saying, "If we're going to be *that* big, maybe we need to redesign our architecture. Maybe we need to redesign our storage." It became a prod for the whole company to better prepare for the future. Everybody started thinking bigger.

Looking back, I doubt we could have reached the goal in four years without the process, structure, and clarity of that stretch OKR. In a fast-growing company, it's a challenge to get everybody to align and focus around the same objective. People need a benchmark to know how they're performing against it. The catch is to find the right one. The billion hours of daily watch time gave our tech people a North Star.

But nothing stays the same. In 2013, the watch-time metric was the best way to gauge the quality of the YouTube experience. Now we're looking at other variables, from web-added videos and photos to viewer satisfaction and a focus on social responsibility. If you watch two videos for ten minutes apiece, the watch time is the same—but which one makes you happier?

So by the time this book is published, we may have found a whole new metric to grow by.

PART TWO

The New World of Work

15

Continuous Performance Management: OKRs and CFRs

Talking can transform minds, which can
transform behaviors, which can transform
institutions.

—*Sheryl Sandberg*

nnual performance reviews are costly, exhausting, and
mostly futile. On average, they swallow 7.5 hours of manager time for each direct report. Yet only 12 percent
of HR leaders deem the process "highly effective" in driving
business value. Only 6 percent think it's worth the time it takes.
Distorted recency bias, burdened by stack rankings and bell
curves, these end-of-year evaluations can't possibly be fair or well
measured.

What business leaders have learned, very painfully, is that individuals cannot be reduced to numbers. Even Peter Drucker, the
champion of well-measured goals, understood the limits of cali-
bration. A manager's "first role," Drucker said, "is the personal

one. It's the relationship with people, the development of mutual confidence . . . the creation of a community." Or as Albert Einstein observed, "Not everything that can be counted counts, and not everything that counts can be counted."

To reach goals almost beyond imagining, people must be managed at a higher level. Our systems for workplace communication cry out for an upgrade. Just as quarterly OKRs have rendered pro forma annual goals obsolete, we need an equivalent tool to revolutionize outdated performance management systems. In short, we need a new HR model for the new world of work. That transformational system, the contemporary alternative to annual reviews, is *continuous performance management*. It is implemented with an instrument called CFRs, for:

- *Conversations*: an authentic, richly textured exchange between manager and contributor, aimed at driving performance

- *Feedback*: bidirectional or networked communication among peers to evaluate progress and guide future improvement

- *Recognition*: expressions of appreciation to deserving individuals for contributions of all sizes

Like OKRs, CFRs champion transparency, accountability, empowerment, and teamwork, at all levels of the organization. As communication stimuli, CFRs ignite OKRs and then boost them into orbit; they're a complete delivery system for measuring what matters. They capture the full richness and power of Andy Grove's innovative method. They give OKRs their human voice.

Best of all, OKRs and CFRs are mutually reinforcing. Doug Dennerline is CEO of BetterWorks, the pioneer in bringing both of these tools to the cloud and smartphones and in helping hundreds of organizations make the processes their own. "It's the marriage between the two—that's the real home run," Doug says. "If a conversation is limited to whether you achieved the goal or not, you lose context. You need continuous performance management to surface the critical questions: Was the goal harder to achieve than you'd thought when you set it? Was it the right goal in the first place? Is it motivating? Should we double down on the two or three things that really worked for us last quarter, or is it time to consider a pivot? You need to elicit those insights from all over the organization.

"On the other hand, if you don't have goals, what the heck are you talking about? What did you achieve, and how? In my experience, people are more likely to feel fulfilled when they have clear and aligned targets. They're not wandering and wondering about their work; they can see how it connects and helps the organization."

To hazard another football analogy: Let's say objectives are the goalposts, the targets you're aiming for, and key results the incremental yard markers for getting there. To flourish as a group, players and coaches need something more, something vital to any collective endeavor. CFRs embody all the interactions that tie the team together from one game to the next. They're the Monday videotape postmortems, the midweek intrasquad meetings, the preplay huddles—and the end-zone celebrations for jobs well done.

Reinventing HR

The good news: A change is in the breeze. Ten percent of Fortune 500 companies have already ditched the old once-a-year performance review system, and their numbers are growing. Countless smaller start-ups, less tied to tradition, are doing the same. We're at the point where nearly every HR custom needs to be reimagined. A mobile, agile workforce—and a nonhierarchical workplace—demands no less.

When companies replace—or at least augment—the annual review with ongoing conversations and real-time feedback, they're better able to make improvements throughout the year. Alignment and transparency become everyday imperatives. When employees are struggling, their managers don't sit and wait for some scheduled day of reckoning. They jump into tough discussions like firefighters, without hesitation.

It might sound almost too easy, but continuous performance management will lift every individual's achievement. It elevates performance, bottom to top. It works wonders for morale and personal development, for leaders and contributors alike. And when leveraged with the quarterly goals and built-in tracking of OKRs, it can be even more powerful.

In this transitional moment, more organizations are broadening their evaluations with alternative criteria, like competencies and team play. Many are now riding parallel tracks, with annual reviews set alongside continuous performance management and ongoing conversations. This balance of old and new thinking can work well for larger companies in particular, some of whom may be happy to live there forever. Others will cut the cord and drop ratings and rankings for more transparent, collaboratively developed, multidimensional review criteria.

Table 15.1: Annual Performance Management Versus Continuous Performance Management

Annual Performance Management	Continuous Performance Management
Annual feedback	Continuous feedback
Tied to compensation	Decoupled from compensation
Directing/autocratic	Coaching/democratic
Outcome focused	Process focused
Weakness based	Strength based
Prone to bias	Fact driven

Continuous Performance Management at Pact

Pact, the Washington, D.C.–based international trade and development nonprofit, has seen firsthand the synergy between OKRs and continuous performance management. Tim Staffa, a Pact director, says:

"We embraced OKRs because our performance management process was moving to a more frequent cadence. When Pact adopted OKRs, we officially killed our annual performance review. We replaced it with a set of more frequent touch points between managers and employees. Internally, we've dubbed this 'Propel.' It consists of four elements:

"The first is a set of monthly one-on-one conversations between employees and their managers about how things are going.

"The second is a quarterly review of progress against our OKRs. We sit down and say, 'What did you set out to accomplish this quarter? What were you able to do—and what weren't you able to do? Why or why not? What can we change?'

"Third, we have a semiannual professional development conversation. Employees talk about their career trajectory—where they've been, where they are, where they want to go. And how their managers and the organization can support their new direction.

"The fourth bit is ongoing, self-driven insight. We're constantly surrounded by positive reinforcement and feedback, but many of us haven't been trained to seek it out. Say you give a presentation to your team. After the fact, somebody comes up to you and says, 'Hey, nice job.' Most of us would say, 'Oh great, thanks,' and move on. But we want to probe a little deeper: 'Thank you. What one thing did you like about it?' The idea is to capture more specific feedback in real time."

An Amicable Divorce

For companies moving to continuous performance management, the first step is blunt and straightforward: Divorce compensation (both raises and bonuses) from OKRs. These should be two distinct conversations, with their own cadences and calendars. The first is a backward-looking assessment, typically held at year's end. The second is an ongoing, forward-looking dialogue between leaders and contributors. It centers on five questions:

What are you working on?

- How are you doing; how are your OKRs coming along?

- Is there anything impeding your work?

- What do you need from me to be (more) successful?

- How do you need to grow to achieve your career goals?

Now, I'm not proposing that performance reviews and goals can or should be completely severed. A data-driven summary of *what* someone has achieved can be a welcome antidote to ratings biases. And since OKRs reflect a person's most meaningful work, they're a source of reliable feedback for the cycle to come. But when goals are used and abused to set compensation, employees can be counted on to sandbag. They start playing defense; they stop stretching for amazing. They get bored for lack of challenge. And the organization suffers most of all.

Let's say Contributor A set extreme stretch goals and somehow attained 75 percent of them. Does her outperformance merit 100 percent of her bonus—or even 120 percent? Contributor B, by contrast, reaches 90 percent of his key results, but his manager knows he didn't push himself—and, what's more, that he blew off several important team meetings. Should he get a larger bonus than Contributor A?

The short answer is no, not if you want to preserve initiative and morale.

At Google, according to Laszlo Bock, OKRs amount to a third or less of performance ratings. They take a backseat to feedback from cross-functional teams, and most of all to context. "It's always possible—even with a goal-setting system—to get the goals wrong," Laszlo says. "Maybe the market does something crazy, or a client leaves their job and suddenly you have to rebuild from scratch. You try to keep all of that in consideration." Google is careful to segregate raw goal scores from compensation decisions. Their OKR numbers are actually wiped from the system after each cycle!

The formula has yet to be invented for complex human behavior, because that's where human judgment comes in. In today's workplace, OKRs and compensation can still be friends. They'll never totally lose touch. But they no longer live together, and it's healthier that way.

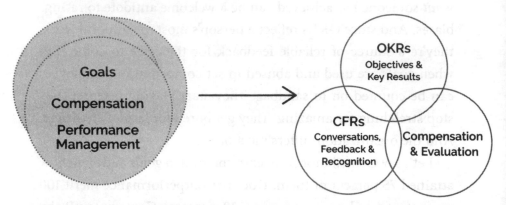

As companies transition to continuous performance management, OKRs and CFRs become mostly independent from compensation and formal evaluations.

Conversations

Peter Drucker was one of the first to stress the value of regular one-on-one meetings between managers and their direct reports. Andy Grove estimated that ninety minutes of a manager's time "can enhance the quality of your subordinate's work for two weeks." Ahead of the curve, as usual, Andy made one-on-ones mandatory at Intel. The point of the meeting, he wrote,

> is mutual teaching and exchange of information. By talking about specific problems and situations, the supervisor teaches the subordinate his skills and know-how, and suggests ways to approach things. At the same time, the subordinate provides the supervisor with detailed information about what he is doing and what he is concerned about. . . . A key point about a

one-on-one: It should be regarded as the subordinate's meeting, with its agenda and tone set by him. . . . The supervisor is there to learn and coach.*

The supervisor should also encourage the discussion of heart-to-heart issues during one-on-ones, because this is the perfect forum for getting at subtle and deep work-related problems affecting his subordinate. Is he satisfied with his own performance? Does some frustration or obstacle gnaw at him? Does he have doubts about where he is going?

With contemporary tools to track and coordinate frequent conversations, Grove's tenets are more timely than ever.† Effective one-on-ones dig beneath the surface of day-to-day work. They have a set cadence, from weekly to quarterly, depending on need. Based on BetterWorks' experience with hundreds of enterprises, five critical areas have emerged of conversation between manager and contributor:

Goal setting and reflection, where the employee's OKR plan is set for the coming cycle. The discussion focuses on how best to align individual objectives and key results with organizational priorities.
Ongoing progress updates, the brief and data-driven check-ins on the employee's real-time progress, with problem solving as needed.‡

---

* Andy believed the "subordinate" should do 90 percent of the talking. When I met with my boss at Intel, he focused on how *he* could help *me* achieve my key results.

† According to Gallup, more frequent one-on-ones increase employee engagement by a factor of three.

‡ Progress updates entail two basic questions: *What's working well? What's not working well?*

Two-way coaching, to help contributors reach their potential and managers do a better job.

Career growth, to develop skills, identify growth opportunities, and expand employees' vision of their future at the company.

Lightweight performance reviews, a feedback mechanism to gather inputs and summarize what the employee has accomplished since the last meeting, in the context of the organization's needs. (*As noted earlier, this conversation is held apart from an employee's annual compensation/bonus review.*)

As workplace conversations become integral, managers are evolving from taskmasters to teachers, coaches, and mentors. Say the head of product has waffled over a design decision, putting a product release date in jeopardy. Before the next executive team meeting, an effective CEO/coach might say, "Can you think about how to be more decisive in this setting? What if you laid out the two best options but made your own preference clear? Do you think you could do that?" If the product head agrees, there is a plan. Unlike negative criticism, coaching trains its sights on future improvement.

Feedback

In her instant classic, *Lean In: Women, Work, and the Will to Lead*, Sheryl Sandberg notes: "Feedback is an opinion, grounded in observations and experiences, which allows us to know what impression we make on others." To reap the full benefits of OKRs, feedback must be integral to the process. If you don't know how well you're performing, how can you possibly get better?

Today's workers "want to be 'empowered' and 'inspired,' not told what to do. They want to provide feedback *to* their managers, not wait for a year to receive feedback *from* their managers. They want to discuss their goals on a regular basis, share them with others, and track progress from peers." Public, transparent OKRs will trigger good questions from all directions: *Are these the right things for me/you/us to be focused on? If I/you/we complete them, will it be seen as a huge success? Do you have any feedback on how I/we could stretch even more?*

Feedback can be highly constructive—but only if it is specific.

Negative feedback: "You started the meeting late last week, and it came off as disorganized."

Positive feedback: "You did a great job with the presentation. You really grabbed their attention with your opening anecdote, and I loved how you closed with next action steps."

In developing organizations, feedback is generally led by HR and often scheduled. In more mature organizations, feedback is ad hoc, real-time, and multidirectional, an open dialogue between people anywhere in the organization. If we can rate our Uber drivers (and vice versa), and even rate the raters on Yelp, why can't a workplace support two-way feedback between managers and employees? Here's the precious opportunity for people to say to their leaders, *What do you need from me to be successful? And now let me tell you what I need from you.*

Not so many years ago, employees made their voices heard by slipping unsigned notes into the office suggestion box. Today, progressive companies have replaced the box with always-on, anonymous feedback tools, from quick-hitting employee surveys to anonymous social networks and even rating apps for meetings and meeting organizers.

Peer-to-peer (or 360-degree) feedback is an added lens for continuous performance management. It can be anonymous or public or somewhere in between. Is the feedback designed to help employees move forward in their careers? (If so, it's channeled privately to the individuals.) Is it meant to reveal an organization's problem areas? (Here it goes straight to HR.) It's all a matter of context and purpose.

By fostering connections among teams, peer feedback is especially valuable in cross-functional initiatives. When horizontal communication blows open, interdepartmental teamwork becomes the new normal. As OKRs are combined with 360-degree feedback, the silo will soon be a relic of the past.

Recognition

Here is the most underestimated component of CFRs, and the least well understood. Gone are the days when gold watches were coveted awards for simple longevity. Modern recognition is performance-based and horizontal. It crowdsources meritocracy. When JetBlue installed a value-driven, peer-to-peer recognition system, and leaders began noticing people who'd flown under their radar, metrics for employee satisfaction nearly doubled.

Continuous recognition is a powerful driver of engagement: "As soft as it seems, saying 'thank you' is an extraordinary tool to building an engaged team. . . . '[H]igh-recognition' companies have 31 percent lower voluntary turnover than companies with poor recognition cultures." Here are some ways to implement it:

* *Institute peer-to-peer recognition.* When employee achievements are consistently recognized by peers, a

culture of gratitude is born. At Zume Pizza, the Friday all-hands "roundup" meeting concludes with a series of unsolicited, unedited shout-outs from anyone in the organization to anyone else who's done something remarkable.

- *Establish clear criteria.* Recognize people for actions and results: completion of special projects, achievement of company goals, demonstrations of company values. Replace "Employee of the Month" with "Achievement of the Month."

- *Share recognition stories.* Newsletters or company blogs can supply the narrative behind the accomplishment, giving recognition more meaning.

- *Make recognition frequent and attainable.* Hail smaller accomplishments, too: that extra effort to meet a deadline, that special polish on a proposal, the little things a manager might take for granted.

- *Tie recognition to company goals and strategies.* Customer service, innovation, teamwork, cost cutting—any organizational priority can be supported by a timely shout-out.

OKR platforms are custom-built for peer-to-peer recognition. Quarterly goals establish and reestablish the areas where feedback and recognition are most valued. Transparent OKRs make it natural for coworkers to celebrate big wins and smaller triumphs alike. All deserve their share of the limelight.

Once teams and departments start connecting in this fashion, more and more people get on board, and a recognition engine revs up an entire company. Anyone can cheer anyone else's goal, irrespective of title or department. And mark this: Every cheer is a step toward operating excellence, the crowning purpose of OKRs and CFRs.

16

Ditching Annual
Performance Reviews:
The Adobe Story

Donna Morris

Executive Vice President
Customer and Employee Experience

Six years ago, like most businesses, the software company Adobe was saddled with antiquated annual performance reviews. Managers invested eight hours per employee and demoralized everyone involved. Voluntary attrition spiked every February, as waves of contributors reacted to disappointing reviews by taking their talent elsewhere. In all, the company devoted a total of eighty thousand manager hours—the equivalent of nearly forty full-time hires—to a mechanical process that created no discernible value. Adobe was transitioning full speed ahead to a cloud-based subscription business model, which it needed to keep winning. But even as the company moved its products and customer relations into a contemporary, real-time operation, its approach to HR remained shackled to the past.

VIRTUAL COMPULSIONS

Adobe Set to Junk Annual Appraisals

Company to rely on regular feedback round the year to rate & reward stuff

DEVINA SENGUPTA
BANGALORE

About 10,000 employees at Adobe Systems, including 2,000 in India, have just completed what could probably be their last performance review. The global product services company plans to scrap the age-old practice of being pitted against colleagues and measured up by the bosses once a year.

"We plan to abolish the performance review format," says Donna Morris, senior VP-HR at the company. Still in its blueprint, the plan is to have managers give regular feedback to their teams to ensure a quicker and continuous self-actualisation, rather than wait for the year end.

Adobe took the plunge after it entered the digital marketing space, which required a completely different gamut of customer base and marketing strategies that called for an overhaul of HR processes as well.

Should Cos Scrap Yearly Reviews?

WHY ...

Once-a-year review may be based on top of mind recall

Regular feedback can help improve performance continuously

Unfair to pit employees against one another in an annual exercise

WHY NOT ...

Difficult to monitor employee's work constantly, especially in virtual teams

Promotions and increments may get complicated

Difficult to get the best out of employees without annual targets and reviews

Jaleel Abdul, HR head for the Indian arm. Not a borrowed practice, the roots can be traced to management guru Marshall Goldsmith's theory on how instant and real-time feedback can boost performance.

"Course correction is also faster and more immediate this way," says Abdul.

Companies constantly innovate and tweak their appraisal systems.

Adobe's leap into the future, as reported in the India Times in 2012.

In 2012, during a business trip to India, an Adobe executive named Donna Morris vented her frustrations over traditional performance management. Her guard lowered by jet lag, she told a reporter that the company planned to abolish annual reviews and stack rankings in favor of more frequent, forward-facing feedback. It was a great idea. The catch was that she hadn't yet discussed it with her HR staff or with Adobe's CEO.

With characteristic energy and persuasiveness, Donna hustled to bring the company around. As she wrote on Adobe's intranet, the challenge at hand was to "review contributions, reward accomplishments, and give and receive feedback. Do they need to be conflated into a cumbersome process? I don't think so. It's time to think radically differently. If we did away with our 'annual review,' what would you like to see in its place? What would it look like to inspire, motivate, and value contributions more effectively?" Her post sparked one of the most widely engaged discussions in company history.

Donna's candor became the catalyst for "Check-in," Adobe's new mode of continuous performance management. In a collective effort to move the company forward, managers, employees, and peers join in multiple Check-in conversations each year. Instead of falling back on the HR team, leaders throughout the organization take proactive ownership of the process.

Lightweight, flexible, and transparent, with minimal structure and no tracking or paperwork, Check-in features three focus areas: quarterly "goals and expectations" (Adobe's term for OKRs), regular feedback, and career development and growth. Sessions are called by contributors and decoupled from compensation. Forced-distribution stack rankings have been replaced by an annual Rewards Check-in. Managers are trained to scale compensation based on employees' performance, their impact on the business, the relative scarcity of their skills, and market conditions. There are no fixed guidelines.

Since the fall of 2012, when Check-in was installed, Adobe's voluntary attrition has dropped sharply. By implementing continuous performance management with CFRs, Adobe has invigorated its entire business operation.*

———

Donna Morris: Adobe was founded on four core values: *genuine, exceptional, innovative,* and *involved.* Our old annual review process contradicted every one of them. So I said to our people: What if there were no ratings and no rankings and no forms? Instead, what if you all knew what was expected of you and had the opportunity to grow your career at Adobe, where each of you is so valued?

Check-in has helped us to live Adobe's values every day. To explain how the new process worked, we kicked it off with the first of a series of thirty-to-sixty-minute web training conferences. We rolled them out to senior leaders, then managers, then employees. (We had a 90 percent employee participation rate.) Each quarter we've addressed a different phase of Check-in, from setting expectations to giving and receiving feedback.

We've also invested in an employee resource center, which offers templates and videos to help our people build their constructive feedback skill set. Adobe has a lot of engineers who weren't necessarily experienced with open dialogue. The center has helped them ease into the process.

Our leaders role-modeled Check-in. They needed to show they were open to feedback themselves, and comfortable being questioned on their vision.

Now we treat every manager as a business leader. They are allocated budgets for base incentives and equity, a pool of money to be distributed as they see fit. It's super-empowering for them to

———

* For more information on the company's fresh approach, I invite you to explore their open source content at www.whatmatters.com/adobe.

Donna Morris speaking at Goal Summit, 2017.

know they are truly responsible for their reports. It's equally empowering for employees to know they have input into the process. By scheduling regular Check-ins through the year, they keep their manager apprised of their progress against action items and goals from prior conversations, along with development needs and ideas for how they might grow. And now that we've done away with fixed pots of compensation, teammates are no longer competitors.

Individuals want to drive their own success. They don't want to wait till the end of the year to be graded. They want to know how they're doing while they're doing it, and also what they need to do differently. Under our new system, our contributors get highly specific performance feedback at least once every six weeks. But in practice it happens every week. Everybody knows where they stand and how they're contributing value to the company. Instead of lagging, the performance management process is leading.

Our feedback under Check-in is often manager-to-employee, but it can be flipped to employee-to-manager: "I felt like I was out on a limb with project X and needed more support." And because Adobe is heavily matrixed, feedback can also be peer-to-peer. In my department, for example, I have a communication partner, a finance partner, and a legal partner. While they report to other people, there are strong dotted lines between us. We review our expectations and give one another feedback on our performance.

From Adobe's experience, I'd say that a continuous performance management system has three requirements. The first is executive support. The second is clarity on company objectives and how they align with individual priorities—as set out in our "goals and expectations," which equate to OKRs. The third is an investment in training to equip managers and leaders to be more effective. We're not shipping people out to courses. We're steering them to one-hour sessions online, with role-played vignettes: "Do you need to give difficult feedback? Here are the steps."

Corrective feedback is naturally difficult for people. But when done well, it's also the greatest gift you can give to someone—because it can change people's mindset and modify their behavior in the most positive, valuable way. We're creating an environment where people say, "You know what? It's okay to make a mistake, because that's how I'm going to grow the most." That's a big part of our culture change.

As Check-in makes clear, HR leaders exist for the success of the business. Our role is to consult with other leaders on how to make all of our constituents successful in fulfilling the company's mission. Success isn't built by forms and rankings and ratings. It's not driven by policies and programs that bog people down and get in their way. The true mechanisms for success are the ones that build capabilities and enable people to deliver for the company.

For a service business, nothing is more valuable than engaged employees who feel they can make a difference and want to stay

Adobe Performance Management, Then and Now

BEFORE: The annual performance review　　　**AFTER: Check-in**

	BEFORE	AFTER
Setting priorities	Employee priorities set at the start of the year and often not revisited.	Priorities set and adjusted with manager regularly.
Feedback process	Long process of submitting accomplishments, soliciting feedback, and writing reviews.	Ongoing process of feedback and dialog with no formal written review of documentation.
Compensation decisions	Onerous process of rating and ranking each employee to determine salary increase and equity.	No formal rating or ranking: manager determines salary and equity annually based on performance.
Cadence of meetings	Feedback sessions inconsistent and not monitored. Spike in employee productivity at the end of the year, timed with performance review discussions.	Feedback conversations expected quarterly, with ongoing feedback becoming the norm. Consistent employee productivity based on ongoing discussions and feedback throughout the year.
HR team role	HR team managed paperwork and processes to ensure all steps were completed.	HR team equips employees and managers to have constructive conversations.
Training and resources	Managed coaching and resources came from HR partners who couldn't always reach everyone.	A centralized Employee Resource Center provides help and answers whenever needed.

Adobe Before-and-After Chart

with the organization. Turnover is costly. The best turnover is internal turnover, where people are growing their careers within your enterprise rather than moving someplace else. People aren't wired to be nomads. They just need to find a place where they feel they can make a real impact. At Adobe, Check-in is making that happen.

17

Baking Better Every Day: The Zume Pizza Story

Julia Collins and Alex Garden
Cofounders and Co-CEOs

A s we've seen, OKRs and CFRs are proven vehicles for high performance and exponential growth. They also have more subtle, internal, quotidian effects—like grooming better executives, or giving less vocal contributors an opportunity to shine. On the long and demanding road to operating excellence, they help organizations improve each and every day. Leaders become better communicators and motivators. Contributors grow into more disciplined, rigorous thinkers. When imbued with meaningful conversations and feedback, structured goal setting teaches people how to work within constraints even as they push against them—an especially critical lesson for smaller, scaling operations.

The Zume Pizza story vividly illustrates these internal dynamics. It's about a start-up using OKRs and CFRs—plus a few robots—to take on the giants of its industry.

For some time now, the $10 billion U.S. pizza delivery market has been controlled by three national chains: Domino's, Pizza

Hut, and Papa John's. They aren't life-altering pizzas, but their brands are well established and own the great advantage of economy of scale. In the spring of 2016, when Zume Pizza opened for business in an out-of-the-way concrete bunker in Silicon Valley, the skeptics came out in droves. "Roboticized, artisanal pizza" was derided as a Left Coast gimmick. The odds for success seemed long.

Going on two years later, Zume is beating those odds by making world-class pizza at a competitive price. The company assigns rote tasks to machines, freeing its people for creative jobs that add more value. Dollars saved on manual labor get plowed into higher-quality ingredients: dough from non-GMO flours, organically grown tomatoes, locally sourced vegetables, and healthfully cured meats. The result is a tastier pie that's actually good for you—and that arrives, still hot, as little as five minutes after you input your order.

As online or mobile app orders link into Zume's conveyor belt, robots stretch and shape the dough, apply the sauce, and safely slide the pizzas into an 800-degree oven. With robotics technology continuing to mature, the company plans to automate the entire process, from adding cheese and custom toppings to loading the partly baked pies into Zume's fleet of algorithmically operated, baking-on the-way trucks. (In the future, there's a fair chance those trucks will be driverless.)

Within three months of launch, Zume had achieved 10 percent market share in its local trade area. In 2018, it began disrupting the pizza oligopoly across the Bay Area. Soon it will roll out across the West Coast, and then nationally; by 2019, the founders hope to be overseas. "We're going to be the Amazon of food," says cofounder Alex Garden, who first met OKRs as president of Zynga Studios.

*Zume cofounders Julia Collins and
Alex Garden with their baking-on-the-way pizza truck.*

When you're David taking on Goliath, time and opportunity are of the essence. There's no margin for unfocused operations or misaligned staff. As Zume's leaders will tell you, OKRs have helped their young company to thrive in ways they could not have foreseen.

———

Julia Collins: In the beginning, Zume lived in our two heads. If you asked Alex and me any question, we would give you the same answer; we spent so much time together that everything was understood. That works fine with two people. After our CTO came on board and we became "the three cheeses," it still worked really well. But once we added Parmigiano-Reggiano to the mozzarella, Romano, and provolone, something changed. By the time we had

A Zume Pizza robot in action.

seven people, if you asked us, "What's the main thing we need to accomplish today?"—well, you'd get eight different answers.

We started with the project management software called LiquidPlanner, a "waterfall" methodology. It really helped build out our kitchen. First you pour the concrete and let it dry; then you put on the epoxy and let that dry; then you cover it and install the walk-in refrigerator box, right? For a linear process, it's fantastic.

But by June 2016, as we prepared to launch, Zume was a more complex operation. We were up to sixteen salaried employees, plus another three dozen hourly kitchen workers and "pilots," the indispensable people who deliver our pizza. We'd ventured into large-scale manufacturing, plus integrating robots, plus developing software, plus creating a menu . . . and the waterfall stopped flowing so smoothly. Too many things were happening at once, with lots of layers of interdependencies. We knew we had to stay agile, and our engineers checked in on JIRA's project management software each morning for their two-week sprints. But neither JIRA nor LiquidPlanner could answer one big question: *What's the most important thing to do?*

Zume's biggest asset is our talented and creative team. Left to their own devices, our folks would jump into what they *thought* was most important. Their ideas were often good but not always in sync. We implemented OKRs early in our life cycle, three weeks after the first pizza went out the door, because we wanted to be sure that everyone knew our top priorities. In the beginning, to make sure that mission-critical things got done, Alex and I set a standard of 100 percent top-down alignment. The two of us created Zume's objectives for our first two OKR cycles. Going forward, as survival becomes less of an issue, we'll loosen up a little bit.

Achieving What's Real

Alex Garden: It's hard to deny the explicit value of OKRs, like how they help tie an organization to the leadership's true ambitions. But for young companies like Zume, especially, there's an equally important *implicit* value that gets overlooked. OKRs are a superb training tool for executives and managers. They teach you how to manage your business within existing limits. It's important to push the envelope, but the envelope is real. *Everybody* faces resource constraints: time, money, people. And the bigger an organization, the more entropy—it's like thermodynamics. During my stint as a general manager at Microsoft's Xbox Live, I worked with some visionary executives. But we struggled from a misalignment between the leaders' desires and the capabilities of the organization. The "hows"—and most of the "whats," as well—were left to me and some other divisional foot soldiers. It was our job to execute an impractically framed mandate for an overscoped mission. If we'd had a well-constructed goal-setting process from the start, it might have saved everyone a lot of grief.

Old-school business models suggest that your role as an executive gets more abstract as you rise in the ranks. Your middle managers buffer you from the operational day-to-day, freeing you to focus on the big picture. Maybe that worked in a slower-paced era. But in my experience, OKRs can't be effective unless the people at the top are unconditionally committed—like a religious calling. And proselytizing is hard and thankless work. Your people may not like you very much through the adoption curve, which can take up to a year. But it's worth it.

Better Discipline

Julia: If we're talking about the intrinsic value of OKRs, what comes before anything is the discipline that they instill in us as co-CEOs.

Alex: They train us to be thoughtful about what we can actually achieve, and to instill the same outlook in our executive team and their teams. Early on in your career, when you're an individual contributor, you're graded on the volume and quality of your work. Then one day, all of a sudden, you're a manager. Let's assume you do well and move up to manage more and more people. Now you're no longer paid for the amount of work you do; you're paid for the quality of decisions you make. But no one tells you the rules have changed. When you hit a wall, you think, I'll just work harder—that's what got me here.

What you *should* do is more counterintuitive: Stop for a moment and shut out the noise. Close your eyes to really see what's in front of you, and then pick the best way forward for you and your team, relative to the organization's needs. What's neat about OKRs is that they formalize reflection. At least once each quarter, they make contributors step back into a quiet place and consider how their decisions align with the company. People start thinking in the macro. They become more pointed and precise, because you can't write a ninety-page OKR dissertation. You have to choose three to five things and exactly how they should be measured. Then when the day comes and someone says, "Okay, you're a manager," you've already learned how to think like one. And that's huge.

Most start-ups aren't too eager to plunge into structured goal setting: *We don't need that. We go super-fast. We just figure stuff out.* And often they do figure it out. But I think they're missing an opportunity to teach people how to be executives *before* the company scales. If those habits aren't ingrained early on, one of two things happens: Unsuccessful companies scale beyond the leadership team's capacity, and they die. Successful companies scale beyond the team's abilities and the team gets replaced. Those are both sad outcomes. The better way is to train people to think like leaders from the start, when their departments have a staff of one.

So OKRs forge your people. They mint stronger executives and help them avoid rookie mistakes. They implant the rigor and rhythm of a very large company into the framework of a very small company. When we implemented OKRs at Zume, the immediate benefit was the process itself. The simple act of forcing people to think about the business—thoughtfully, transparently, interdependently—was a huge accelerant to their performance.

Better Engagement

Alex: OKRs take out the ambiguity. And when you do that, some people will say, "This isn't what I thought I signed up for, and I'm leaving." But others will say, "I'm inspired because I finally know what we're trying to do." Either way, there's clarity. For those who stay, you've laid the foundation for engagement. Everybody's bought in to the mission. Team sports don't work unless the whole team plays together.

Julia: As people get more familiar with the OKR process, it naturally gets more collaborative. In Q3 of 2016, Alex and I wrote the top company OKRs, and the department heads converted some of our key results into their own objectives. We just cascaded them down. In Q4, the two of us still wrote the company objectives, but our team jumped in and KRed them from the top, which was great. They took on a more creative role, and the OKRs got better. Our goals were still stretched, but people felt they were more realistic.

Zume calls its key technology "baking on the way." That's where we disrupt the industry and create the most delight for our customers. In Q4, a top company objective was to deploy our big guys, the twenty-six-foot trucks with fifty-six ovens linked to a sophisticated logistics and order prediction system. They enable us to finish your pizza algorithmically, in as little as five minutes after your online order, and have it ready—and still steaming—as we pull up to your door. Vaibhav Goel, our product manager, owned an OKR to order, coordinate, and fulfill the first flotilla of our baking-on-the-way fleet. It was airtight. If Vaibhav attained his three KRs, we knew we'd reach our objective.

> ## OBJECTIVE
> **Complete the Truck Delivery Fleet for 250 Polaris (Mountain View HQ).**
>
> ### KEY RESULTS
> 1. **Deliver 126 fully certified ovens by 11/30.**
> 2. **Deliver 11 fully certified racks by 11/30.**
> 3. **Deliver 2 fully certified full-format delivery vehicles by 11/30.**

Every organization has people who are more vocal in asserting themselves. If they don't win their point the first time, they're comfortable saying it again. But quieter folks may not be heard so well, and their needs can get neglected. The OKR framework gives equal voice and weight to each department. No one needs to suffer in silence—truthfully, no one has that option. Your objectives will get their turn up on the screen, like everyone else's, for comment and support.

I'd add that a really good company values different opinions. It mines for dissent, and it finds a way to bring it up to the surface and mine it out. That's how we foster a meritocracy.

Alex: Before rolling OKRs out to our individual contributors, we put in two full quarters at the exec level. We had to establish the culture first. What we've found, oddly enough, is that our most active participants are the ones who were initially most skeptical.

Joseph Suzuki (director of marketing): I thought it another diet program—*Just follow this process and you'll be thin and beautiful.* It felt like bookkeeping, one more administrative exercise. But OKRs had an effect on me I didn't expect. When I did my biweekly check-ins, it gave me a couple minutes to think about what I was doing, and how my goals rolled up to what the company needed for the quarter.

At a start-up, you can get lost in tactical minutiae—especially in my department, where we wear so many hats. That's dangerous, because you're swimming in tumultuous seas and it's easy to lose sight of land. But those OKR meditations helped me reset my compass: *How do I contribute to the scheme of things?* Then it's not just another report or campaign or field event. It connects to something bigger and more meaningful.

Better Transparency

Julia: From the beginning, the process forced us to clarify who's in charge of what. When a fly ball is hit between two outfielders, somebody's got to call for it—or else the ball drops in, or both people dive for it and crash into each other. Early on, our fielders were marketing and product—but who was responsible for Zume's revenue targets? The two leads had been with us one month apiece. Not only were they new to OKRs, but they were also new to Zume, and Zume was new to itself. When Alex and I saw their confusion, we broke the objective out into new revenue (marketing) and repeat revenue (product), and the department heads drilled down from there. That was an important conversation. It wasn't linked to an objective, per se, but it was absolutely a by-product of an early-stage OKR process. When something isn't clearly delineated, it shows up right away. You can't miss it.

Better Teamwork

Alex: In eight months we launched a food company, a logistics company, a robotics company, and a manufacturing company—from a standing start. We used OKRs as a teaching tool to impart a culture of consideration. They make you start thinking reflexively about how the work you're doing affects those around you, and how you're dependent on them, too.

Julia: Our team is very eclectic. Our executive chef, Aaron Butkus, came up through mom-and-pop restaurants around New York City. Our fleet manager, Mike Bessoni, worked in movie production. We've got a product wonk and a software engineer, and everyone came in speaking different languages. OKRs were our Esperanto, our shared vocabulary. The seven-member leadership team meets over lunch every Monday, and about every other week we discuss our OKRs. You hear people saying things like "Who owns the customer?" or "How would you key-result that goal?" And everyone knows just what they mean.

The most delicious pie in the world won't make people happy if it gets to them cold. Mike and Aaron own a shared objective for customer satisfaction. Mike might say, "I've got a key result for expanding our delivery radius, and now it's at risk." Maybe the manufacturing team was delayed in getting a vehicle online. So now we'll have a collective conversation on how the late deployment is affecting our service area and revenue stream. Which also ties in to Joe Suzuki, our marketing lead, and his OKR to increase top-line revenue.

In another life, Mike might have called out the manufacturing lead: "What the hell, can you hurry up and get this done? I've been waiting forever!" When you say instead, "My KR is at risk," it's less charged and more constructive. Since our company has total align-ment, the entire team has already agreed to the key result and the dependency it entails. There's no judgment, just a problem to be solved. And guess what else happens? The two leads will advocate *for each other* to get more resources from Alex and me.

Aaron Butkus (executive chef): If I'm creating a new seasonal pie, I can't do it on the spur. Marketing needs to know at least a week ahead of time, and then photo and design have to take pictures. It affects every department—the product manager's web-site, the tech team and their mobile app. The OKRs keep me cen-tered and on track. They guarantee that I get the recipe done in time for everyone who's waiting on it. My deadline's built into a key result. I can see the bigger picture more clearly.

It's definitely a team-building process. It reminds you that you're a part of this little, weird community. It's easy to get caught up in your own issues, especially when you're working in the kitchen. But OKRs get people to think, Oh yeah, we're working together on this, we're working together on everything.

Better Conversations

Alex: Every two weeks, each person at Zume has a one-hour, one-on-one conversation with whomever they report to. (Julia and I converse with each other.) It's a sacred time. You cannot be late; you cannot cancel. There's only one other rule: You don't talk about work. The agenda is you, the individual, and what you are trying to accomplish personally over the next two to three years, and how you're breaking that into a two-week plan. I like to start with three questions: *What makes you very happy? What saps your energy? How would you describe your dream job?*

Then I say, "Look, I want to tell you what my expectations are. Number one, always tell the truth. Number two, always do the right thing. If you meet those expectations, we'll unconditionally back you, one hundred percent of the time. And I will personally guarantee you that you're going to achieve your next set of personal and professional goals over the next three years." And we go from there.

People might see this as altruism, but it's actually a powerful way to get people connected to the business—and to keep them from churning out. It gives them insights around obstacles. A leader might say, "This goal seems very important to you, but you didn't make a lot of progress on it the last two weeks. Why is that?" It may seem paradoxical, but these nonwork, touchpoint one-on-ones are a forum for ongoing performance feedback. In talking about people's pursuit of personal goals, you end up learning a lot about what moves them forward—or holds them back—in their careers.

When you're having regular, deeper conversations, you get a sense of when you need to turn the dial and give people a chance to charge their batteries. After the organization has completed an all-out sprint, you might dial up contributors' time for personal development goals—say, from 5 percent to 15 or 20 percent—the next quarter. It might sound like a huge tax, but it will set up the company's two or three quarters of execution.

Better Culture

Julia: Culture is the common language that allows for individuals in an organization to be sure they're all talking about the same thing—and that what they're talking about has meaning. Beyond that, culture establishes a common framework for decision making. In its absence, people are at a loss for how to make key functions replicable and scalable.

Then there's the more aspirational layer of culture: the values conversation. Who do we want to be as an organization? How do we want people to feel about their work, and about our product? What's the impact we want to make on the world?

Alex: Zume's founding principles—our mission—are two things Julia said to me on the phone when we were first introduced. They made such an impression on me that we put them up on a giant poster on our kitchen wall. The first was: *Serving food to people is a sacred trust.* And the second: *Every American has a right to delicious, affordable, healthy food.*

Here's an OKR that flowed directly from our mission:

OBJECTIVE

Delight customers.

DETAIL

Feeding people is a sacred trust. To maintain that trust, we have to deliver the very best customer service and the very best food quality. To succeed as business, we must ensure that our customers are so happy with our service and product that they have no choice but to order more pizza and to rave about the experience with their friends.

KEY RESULTS

1. Net Promoter Score of 42 or better.
2. Order Rating of 4.6/5.0 or better.
3. 75% of customers prefer Zume to competitor in blind taste test.

Julia: There are so many daily decisions that are governed by our mission. It would be easy to use a tiny bit more salt in our pizzas. Or add a little bit of sugar to the sauce rather than going the extra mile to find the freshest tomatoes. Those are the small, insidious compromises that can creep into an organization and undermine who you are.

Every new employee goes through mission and values training as part of their onboarding. Alex and I are very clear about what we expect from people. And our clarity forces us to be highly accountable, as an organization and as individuals. We have a best-idea-wins culture, and people are free to call out anybody, including the CEO.

Alex: Especially the CEO, that's the best call-out there is. When people challenge us in an open forum, we always stop and make a huge big deal about how impressive it is that the person spoke up. We try to overdo it, to create permission for people to lean in.

Better Leaders

Julia: I've worked for some great leaders in my day. They were all very different, but one thing they had in common was this cold, sober focus. If you sat down with them for twenty minutes, they were completely uncluttered in their thinking. They could drill down very clearly on what needed to be done. When you're fundraising and making pizza with robots and building out kitchens, there's a lot of rapid context switching. It can feel a little frenetic at times. But when you know your company objectives like you know your last name, it's very calming. OKRs help me to be that focused, clear-headed leader. No matter how crazy things get, I can always default back to what matters.

18

Culture

You need a culture that high-fives small and
innovative ideas.

—*Jeff Bezos*

Culture, as the saying goes, eats strategy for breakfast. It's
our stake in the ground; it's what makes meaning of work.
Leaders are rightly obsessed with culture. Founders ask
how they can protect their companies' cultural values as they
grow. Chiefs of large companies are turning to OKRs and CFRs as
tools for culture change. And growing numbers of job seekers and
career builders are making the right cultural fit their top criterion.

As you have seen throughout this book, OKRs are clear vessels
for leaders' priorities and insights. CFRs help ensure that those
priorities and insights get transmitted. But goals cannot be attained in a vacuum. Like sound waves, they require a medium.
For OKRs and CFRs, the medium is an organization's culture, the
living expression of its most cherished values and beliefs.

And so the question becomes: How do companies define and
build a positive culture? While I have no simple answer, OKRs
and CFRs provide a blueprint. By aligning teams to work toward

a handful of common objectives, then uniting them through lightweight, goal-oriented communications, OKRs and CFRs create transparency and accountability, the tent poles for sustained high performance. Healthy culture and structured goal setting are interdependent. They're natural partners in the quest for operating excellence.

Andy Grove understood the paramount importance of this interplay. "Put simply," he wrote in *High Output Management*, culture is "a set of values and beliefs, as well as familiarity with the way things are done and should be done in a company. The point is that a strong and positive corporate culture is absolutely essential." As an engineer, Grove equated culture with efficiency, a manual for quicker, more reliable decisions. When a company is culturally coherent, the way forward is understood:

> Someone adhering to the values of a corporate culture—an intelligent corporate citizen—will behave in consistent fashion under similar conditions, which means that managers don't have to suffer the inefficiencies engendered by formal rules, procedures, and regulations. . . . [M]anagement has to develop and nurture the common set of values, objectives, and methods essential to the existence of trust. How do we do that? One way is by articulation, by spelling [them] out. . . . The other even more important way is by example.

As an executive, Grove role-modeled Intel's highest cultural standards. In his iOPEC seminars, he endeavored to instill them in the company's new employees. On the following page you'll find two original slides from 1985, an outline of Andy's teachings on Intel's seven core cultural values:

Operating Style
– Our Value System

- **People oriented**
  - we value a strong mutual commitment
  - respect for all work
  - challenge and opportunity

- **Openness**
  - highlighting of problems or issues expected

- **Issue resolution**
  - clean and crisp
  - confrontation must be constructive

- **Results**
  - output orientation in all work
  - superficiality not respected
  - reward successes with positive feedback

IOPEC

- **Discipline**
  - excellence in a highly competitive, complex environment demands it

- **Risk taking**
  - high technology orientation necessitates it
  - low fear of failing, self-exposure
  - champions

- **Trust and integrity**

IOPEC

Intel Slide—Operating Style

The qualities prized by Andy Grove—collective accountability, fearless risk taking, measurable achievement—are also highly esteemed at Google. In Project Aristotle, an internal Google study of 180 teams, standout performance correlated to affirmative responses to these five questions:

1. **Structure and clarity:** Are goals, roles, and execution plans on our team clear?
2. **Psychological safety:** Can we take risks on this team without feeling insecure or embarrassed?
3. **Meaning of work:** Are we working on something that is personally important for each of us?
4. **Dependability:** Can we count on each other to do high-quality work on time?
5. **Impact of work:** Do we fundamentally believe that the work we're doing matters?

The first item on this list—structure and clarity—is the raison d'être for objectives and key results. The others are all key facets of a healthy workplace culture, and tie directly to OKR superpowers and CFR communication tools. Consider peer-to-peer "dependability." In a high-functioning OKR environment, transparency and alignment make people more diligent in meeting their obligations. At Google, teams assume collective responsibility for goal achievement—or for failures. At the same time, individuals are held responsible for specific key results. Peak performance is the product of collaboration *and accountability.*

An OKR culture is an accountable culture. You don't push toward a goal just because the boss gave you an order. You do it because every OKR is transparently important to the company, and to the colleagues who count on you. Nobody wants to be seen as the one holding back the team. Everybody takes pride in moving progress forward. It's a social contract, but a self-governed one.

———

In *The Progress Principle*, Teresa Amabile and Steven Kramer analyzed 26 project teams, 238 individuals, and 12,000 employee diary entries. High-motivation cultures, they concluded, rely on a mix of two elements. *Catalysts*, defined as "actions that support work," sound much like OKRs: "They include setting clear goals, allowing autonomy, providing sufficient resources and time, helping with the work, openly learning from problems and successes, and allowing a free exchange of ideas." *Nourishers*—"acts of interpersonal support"—bear a striking resemblance to CFRs: "respect and recognition, encouragement, emotional comfort, and opportunities for affiliation."

In the high-stakes arena of culture change, OKRs lend us purpose and clarity as we plunge into the new. CFRs supply the energy we need for the journey. Where people have authentic conversations and get constructive feedback and recognition for superior accomplishment, enthusiasm becomes infectious. The same goes for stretch thinking and a commitment to daily improvement. The companies that treat their people as valued partners are the ones with the best customer service. They have the best products and strongest sales growth. They're the ones who are going to win.

As continuous performance management rises to the fore, once-a-year employee surveys are giving way to real-time feedback. One frontier is *pulsing*, an online snapshot of your workplace culture. These signal-capturing questionnaires may be scheduled weekly or monthly by HR or made part of an ongoing "drip" campaign. Either way, pulses are simple, quick, and wide-ranging. For example: *Are you getting enough sleep? Have you met recently with your manager to discuss goals and expectations? Do you have a clear sense of your career path? Are you getting enough challenge and motivation and energy—are you feeling "in the zone"?*

Feedback is a listening system. In the new world of work, leaders cannot wait for negative critiques on Glassdoor, or for valued contributors to exit for another job. They need to listen and capture signals as they are emitted. What if a goal-setting platform could pulse two or three questions to employees whenever they log in? What if it merged quantitative data on goal progress with qualitative input from frequent conversations and pulsing feedback? We're not far away from software that will prompt a manager: "Talk to Bob, something's going on with his team."

As OKRs build goal muscle, CFRs make those sinews more flexible and responsive. Pulsing gauges the organization's real-time health—body and soul, work and culture.

———

Leading the world in online higher education, Coursera jumped into OKRs in 2013, just one year after its founding. With timely input from then-president Lila Ibrahim, an Intel alumna who revered Andy Grove, the organization tried something rare and exemplary. They connected OKRs explicitly to the company's values and lofty mission statement, a clear expression of its culture: "We envision a world where anyone, anywhere, can transform their lives by accessing the world's best learning experience." Coursera rolled up its team-level objectives to top-line strategic objectives, which in turn rolled up to five core values:

- *Students first.* Engage and increase value to students; extend reach to new students.

- *Great partners.* Be a great partner to universities.

- *Think big and advance pedagogy.* Develop an innovative, world-class education platform.

- *Care for teammates and be human, be humble.* Build a strong, healthy organization.

- *Do good, do well.* Experiment and develop a sustainable business model.

Each core value was mapped to a corresponding set of OKRs. As an example, here is an OKR for "students first":

> ### OBJECTIVE
> **Extend Coursera's reach to new students.**
>
> ### KEY RESULTS
> 1. **Perform A/B tests, learn, and iterate on ways to acquire new students and engage existing students.**
> 2. **Increase mobile monthly active users (MAU) to 150k.**
> 3. **Create internal tools to track key growth metrics.**
> 4. **Launch features to enable instructors to create more engaging videos.**

OKRs furnished the pathway for Coursera's mission. They enabled teams to articulate their goals and to align with the company's objectives—and with its broader values, as well. Years later, the company's friendly, inclusive culture remains a welcome contrast to the blustery, combative personality of many Silicon Valley start-ups.

Coursera team with former president and COO Lila Ibrahim (left),
cofounder Daphne Kohler (to the left of John Doerr), and cofounder
Andrew Ng (far right), 2012.

As Rick Levin, Coursera's former CEO, said, "I can't imagine where we would be without OKRs. The discipline forces us to look back every quarter and hold ourselves accountable, and to look ahead every quarter to imagine how we can better live our values."

———

In 2007, the preeminent business philosopher Dov Seidman published a groundbreaking book on culture, *HOW: Why HOW We Do Anything Means Everything . . . in Business (and in Life)*. Dov started from the premise that culture guides people's behaviors, or how things really happen in an organization. In our open-sourced, hyperconnected world, behavior defines a company more meaningfully than product lines or market share. As Dov said to me recently, "It's the one thing that can't be copied or commoditized."

Dov's big idea is that companies that "out-behave" their competition will also outperform them. He identified a value-driven model, the "self-governing organization," a place where long-term legacy trumps the next quarter's ROI. These organizations don't merely engage their workers. They *inspire* them. They replace rules with shared principles; carrots and sticks are supplanted by a common sense of purpose. They are built around trust, which enables risk taking, which spurs innovation, which drives performance and productivity.

"In the past," Dov told me, "when employees just needed to do the next thing right—to follow orders to the letter—culture didn't matter so much. But now we're living in a world where we're asking people to do *the next right thing*. A rulebook can tell me what I can or can't do. I need culture to tell me what I *should* do."

That was a majestic, potentially transformative idea. But as Dov has acknowledged, it's one thing to proclaim values like courage or compassion or creativity. It's another to scale them. Scaling requires a system, with metrics. "What we choose to measure is a window into our values, and into *what* we value," Dov says. "Because if you measure something, you're telling people that it matters."

To validate his argument and test his observations, Dov needed data—lots of it. His team at LRN embarked upon a rigorous empirical analysis that has been refined over the years and published in a series of annual HOW reports.

Where Andy Grove added qualitative goals to balance quantitative ones, Dov has found a way to quantify seemingly abstract values like trust. His "trust index" measures specific behaviors—the direct "hows" of transparency, for example. "I avoid asking people about their perceptions," Dov told me. "I don't ask, 'Do you feel your company is honest with you?' I look at information flows. Does the company hoard information, does it mete it out on a need-to-know basis, or is it flowing freely? If you go around your boss and talk to somebody more senior, are you punished or celebrated?"

As of 2016, the HOW report covered seventeen countries and more than sixteen thousand employees. It found that self-governing organizations had grown to 8 percent of the pie, up from 3 percent in 2012. Of those value-driven companies, 96 percent scored high in systematic innovation. Ninety-five percent had superior employee engagement and loyalty. "Out-behavior" did indeed equate to outperformance; 94 percent reported increased market share.

When Dov told me there was no more powerful cultural force than "active transparency," where "human beings are opening up, sharing the truth, bringing others in, being vulnerable," I could see Andy Grove smiling. An OKR/CFR culture is above all a transparent culture. It goes back to the lessons I first learned at Intel, and have seen affirmed countless times at Google and dozens of other forward-looking companies. Vision-based leadership beats command-and-control. The flatter the org chart, the more agile the organization. When performance management is a networked, two-way street, individuals grow into greatness.

At the end, it's all about knitting ourselves to one another. As Dov observes, "Collaboration itself—our ability to *connect*—is an engine of growth and innovation."

Given the chance, OKRs and CFRs will build top-down alignment, team-first networking, and bottom-up autonomy and engagement—the pillars of any vibrant, value-driven culture. But in some scenarios, as you're about to see in the following tale about Lumeris, culture change may need to be initiated *before*

OKRs are deployed. In others, as Bono and his ONE Campaign will show, a charismatic CEO/founder (in this case, a literal rock star) can call on OKRs to transform culture from the top. And so our final two stories explore this rich interrelationship between culture change and structured goal setting.

19

Culture Change:
The Lumeris Story

Andrew Cole

Chief HR/Organizational Development Officer

When an organization isn't yet ready for total openness and accountability, culture work may be needed before OKRs are implemented. As Jim Collins observes in *Good to Great*, first you need to get "the right people on the bus, the wrong people off the bus, and the right people in the right seats." Only then do you turn the wheel and step on the gas.

Not too long ago, a leader in value-based health care stood at a crossroads. Lumeris is a St. Louis–based technology and solutions firm that provides software, services, and know-how to health care providers and payers. Its clientele ranges from university hospital networks to traditional insurers. The company had started in 2006 by partnering with a group of 200 St. Louis–area physicians through a federally regulated insurance company, Essence Healthcare, to serve 65,000 Missouri seniors with a Medicare Advantage plan.

Tapping into a vast trove of patient data, Lumeris helps partner organizations convert traditional, fee-for-service, volume-based "sick care" into something else entirely: a health care delivery system that incentivizes prevention and discourages needless tests or detrimental hospital stays. Under this value-based model, primary-care doctors take responsibility for their patients, cradle to grave. The goal is to improve quality of life while conserving precious resources and dollars. At Lumeris they've shown how those objectives can work hand in hand.

According to CEO Mike Long, the moonshot goal is to rationalize the nation's health care supply chain: "In every other industry, success is based on transparent cost, quality, service, and the availability of choices. None of those principles work in health care, because the system is completely opaque. Doctors have difficulty knowing what services are requisitioned on your behalf, much less what they cost. So how then can you hold them accountable for financial outcomes?" It's a transformational challenge, and Lumeris—aided by OKRs—is leading the charge.

Given its reliance on transparent data, Lumeris seemed a natural fit for Andy Grove's goal-setting system. But as Andrew Cole, the former head of HR, will tell you, adaptation was anything but simple. If cultural barriers go unaddressed, as Andrew says, "The antibodies will be set loose and the body will reject the donor organ of OKRs." As an experienced architect of sweeping organizational change, Andrew was the right person in the right seat to make sure the OKR transplant took.

———

Andrew Cole: When I came to Lumeris, they had been working with OKRs for three quarterly cycles—on paper. They had an outstanding employee participation rate, or so I was told. But after a deep-dive analysis, I realized the process was superficial. At the end of the quarter, a lone HR person ran around like a Jack Russell, nipping at managers' heels to get updated numbers before the board meeting. People dropped into the software platform, conveniently adjusted an objective's metrics, and said, "Oh yeah, I got that done." They'd slap on a date and check off a box. It looked great on PowerPoint, but it wasn't real.

Few of our people understood the business rationale behind OKRs. We were missing explicit buy-in from executive leadership. Most of all, nobody held anybody accountable for getting the system right. When I examined people's objectives, they weren't connected to the actual work. I'd go to managers and ask, "Why does this show up in your OKRs?" In many cases, they had no idea how their objectives linked up to what we were working to achieve. It was so much window dressing.

I try to understand an organization before I charge in, breaking things. But two quarters later, I still wasn't sure the OKR process could be saved. In a closed board session, I asked John Doerr, "If I don't think this tool is right for us, then we won't do it, right?" And he said, "Absolutely." By then I'd diagnosed our root problem, a passive-aggressive approach. No one had addressed a basic question everyone at Lumeris was asking: "What's in this for me?" Though the OKR program was sincerely intended to improve goal setting and collaborative communication, people didn't trust it. Unless we changed the environment, it couldn't possibly succeed.

Transformation doesn't happen overnight. The executive team had brought in OKRs to help integrate two clashing internal cultures. Essence, the health insurance company formed by the St. Louis doctors' group, was risk averse, per Hippocrates; Lumeris pushed to the edge to find the next big tech and data insights. Essence nurtured a proprietary model within a hypercompetitive industry; Lumeris took those learnings and shared them with the world.

As demand for our services began surging, this culture gap was slowing us down. In May 2015, eleven weeks after I arrived, we announced a total reorganization under the Lumeris umbrella. (One company, our reasoning went, should have one name.) I knew that OKRs could eventually be our lingua franca, a way to connect everyone's goals, but that would need to wait. Without cultural alignment, the world's best operational strategy will fail.

HR Transformation

People watch what you do more than what you say. Lumeris had some senior leaders with an old-school, autocratic approach. They weren't living our core values: ownership, accountability, passion for the job, loyalty to the team. Nothing else would matter until those leaders exited the organization. We made sure they left us with their dignity and respect intact, a telling moment in any transformation project.

At each and every culture meeting, we told our employees: "You have the right—no, the obligation—to hold your executive team accountable for what we're saying our culture should be. If we're not following through, make an appointment or send an email. Or just walk up to us in the hallway and tell us we are not getting it done."

It took three months for anyone to take us up on our invitation. Our CEO, Mike Long, engaged with a lunch group and said, "Why would anybody want to work in an environment with a fear of holding each other accountable?" That was a powerful inflection point, and people began to believe. But culture change can be very personal. It took one conversation at a time to convince our employees that collaboration, shared accountability, and transparency would be rewarded. And to show they had nothing to fear from the new Lumeris.

HR can be a potent vehicle for operating excellence. It's also the place where culture change is crystallized—at the end of the day, culture is about the people you recruit and the values they bring to bear. While Lumeris had its share of A and B players in middle management, there were also C players and below who'd been hired with erroneous criteria and vague interviews. There is no tool, OKRs included, that will work with the wrong instruction manual.

Time is the enemy of transformation. We took less than eighteen months to replace 85 percent of our HR professionals. Once senior management and frontline employees were fully on board, we tackled the tougher nut: strengthening middle management. That's typically a three-year process, from start to steady state. When it's complete, your new culture is assured.

OBJECTIVE

Institute a culture that attracts and retains a players.

KEY RESULTS

1. Focus on hiring A player managers/leaders.
2. Optimize recruitment function to attract A player talent.
3. Scrub all job descriptions.
4. Retrain everyone engaged in the interviewing process.
5. Ensure ongoing mentoring/coaching opportunities.
6. Create a culture of learning for development of new and existing employees.

OKR Resurrection

Late in 2015, I asked my HR team to dissect the company's earlier stab at OKRs. If we were to make another go of it, we'd need to retrain everybody in the company—and I meant everybody. We wouldn't get a third chance.

The following April, we relaunched the platform with a sixty-day pilot program for a hundred employees in our operations group. Our senior vice president for operations and delivery, had his doubts going in. But with sharpened training, plus improvements to the software, he became an enthusiast. Within less than two weeks, he was shooting emails to the pilot group: *Why did you write this objective that way? What's the metric here? I don't get this OKR, it isn't what I'm seeing from client feedback.* And his people were thinking, He's paying attention! I'd better look at this more closely.

Winning our troops over to OKRs wasn't easy or instantaneous, far from it. Transparency is scary. Admitting your failures—visibly, publicly—can be terrifying. We had to rewire people from how they'd been raised since kindergarten. It's like your first scuba dive, when you go thirty-five feet down and the adrenaline is pumping and you're scared out of your wits. But when you come back up, you're exhilarated. You have a new insight into how things work beneath the surface.

It's no different plunging into OKRs. Once you start having honest, vulnerable, two-way conversations with your direct reports, you begin to see what makes them tick. You feel their yearning to connect to things bigger than themselves. You hear their need for recognition that what they're doing matters. Through the open window of objectives and key results, each of you gets to know the other's weaknesses with no worry of getting caught out. (For managers, one particular benefit of OKRs is to lead them to hires who can compensate for their own limitations.) Our people stopped dancing around their setbacks. They began to realize there was no shame in trying your hardest and failing, not when OKRs help you fail smart and fail fast.

The tide turned. We began hearing comments like "I was a complete naysayer, but now I see how this can work for me." Ninety-eight percent of the pilot group became active users of our OKR platform; 72 percent set at least one objective aligned to the company's goals. And 92 percent of the pilot group said they now understood "what my manager expects of me."

Transparency Without Judgment

By then I was working with Art Glasgow, who came on board in the spring of 2016 as our president and COO. The two of us agreed there was no point to OKRs unless we went all the way. Art volunteered to be executive sponsor, our goal-setting shepherd. He stood up in front of an all-hands meeting and said, "OKRs are how we're going to run the company, and we're going to use them to measure your bosses." (That was the carrot that balanced the stick.) Art's role in the crusade cannot be overestimated. He set the tone for what he calls "brutal transparency without judgment." And he made my job less lonely.

In Q3, as OKRs were rolled out to all 800 Lumeris employees, we created our own coaches' training program. Over a period of five weeks, our reinvented HR department worked overtime to meet with every single manager—more than 250 of them—in classroom-size groups. We held open houses for them to come and talk to us one-on-one, and we told them up front there were no dumb questions. Those sessions became a golden opportunity. They were instrumental in building engagement and motivating people to deliver against expectations.

Goal setting is more art than science. We weren't just teaching people how to refine an objective or a measurable key result. We had a cultural agenda, as well.

- *Why* is transparency important? Why would you want people across other departments to know your goals? And why does what we're doing matter?

- *What* is true accountability? What's the difference between accountability with respect (for others' failings) and accountability with vulnerability (for our own)?

- *How* can OKRs help managers "get work done through others"? (That's a big factor for scalability in a growing company.) How do we engage other teams to adopt our objective as a priority and help assure that we reach it?

- *When* is it time to stretch a team's workload—or to ease off on the throttle? When do you shift an objective to a different team member, or rewrite a goal to make it clearer, or remove it completely? In building contributors' confidence, timing is everything.

There is no handbook to address these questions. The wisdom resides in leaders with personal connections to their teams, to managers who can show what success looks like and know when to declare victory. (My advice: Not too soon.)

Our training investment paid dividends. In Q3 of 2016, our people's first full crack at the system, 75 percent of them created at least one OKR. Our retention numbers began moving in the right direction. Lumeris has fewer involuntary exits these days. We're hiring the right people and keeping the ones who can thrive here.

Selling Your Reds

Shortly after arriving, Art held a full-day, off-site business review for the Lumeris leadership team. Now it's on the company's monthly calendar. When our top-line OKRs are projected on a screen, it's clear to see which leaders are making their objectives. Art doesn't like yellows, so every OKR is either green (on track) or red (at risk). There's no bell-curve ambiguity, no place for problems to hide.

The reviews run for three hours, with a dozen senior executives taking their turn. Little time is spent on people's greens. Instead, they "sell" their reds. The team votes on the most important at-risk OKRs for the company as a whole, then brainstorms together as long as it takes to get the objectives back on track. In the spirit of cross-departmental solidarity, individuals volunteer to "buy" their colleagues' reds. As Art says, "We're all here to help. We're all in the same bathwater." As far as I know, "selling your reds" is a unique use of OKRs, and one well worth emulating.

Today's transformed Lumeris values interdependence. It prizes intentional coordination. "OKRs make you focus on working *on* the business, instead of just working *in* the business," says Jeff Smith, senior vice president for U.S. markets. "Our regional market heads are quarterbacking opportunities versus running them solo. We're moving from hero culture to team culture." Smith was happily surprised to find the operations and delivery team tying their objectives directly to Smith's sales goals. In the past, Smith said, "You'd hear things like, 'I'm in delivery, you're in sales, just do your damn job.' Now it's more like calling in a wide receiver to run a play: 'I'm here, let me help you.' That was a result of the OKR process I never expected."

First, Lumeris needed to nurture the right culture for OKRs to take root. Then it needed OKRs to sustain and deepen that new culture, to help it win people's hearts and minds. That's a campaign that never ends.

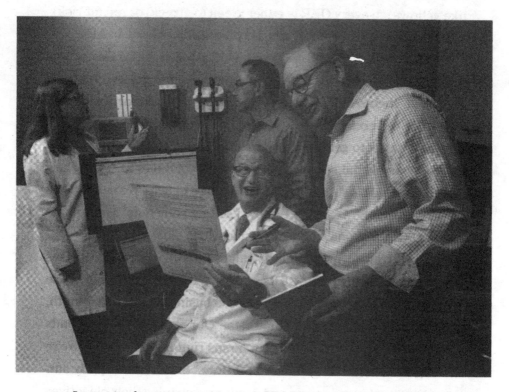

Lumeris physicians and leaders, 2017. Rear: Dr. Susan Adams, COO Art Glasgow. Front: Dr. Tom Hastings, CEO Mike Long.

———

By all the metrics, 2017 was a banner year for Lumeris, now the market leader for value-based care. "The market's starting to shift," Art Glasgow told me. "For the first time I feel like our sales plan could start to get realistic. I might actually have to put in some stretch goals."

As of this writing, Lumeris has launched partnerships with payers, provider groups, and health systems in eighteen states, accounting for more than one million lives. The potential is staggering. If adopted nationwide, the company's Missouri model could save up to $800 billion annually in wasteful medical expenditures. Most important, it would enhance our nation's quality and quantity of life.

At today's Lumeris, OKRs are part of the wallpaper. As Andrew Cole might say: Once people experienced the new company under the surface, they couldn't resist the temptation to keep diving back into it.

20

Culture Change:
Bono's ONE Campaign Story

Bono
Cofounder

We've just seen how OKRs can lock in culture change post hoc. As Bono's story shows structured goal setting can also springboard an enriching cultural reset.

For nearly two decades, the world's biggest rock star has waged "an experiment in anti-apathy on a global scale." Bono's first Big Hairy Audacious Goal came out of the Jubilee 2000 global initiative, which led to $100 billion in debt relief for the world's poorest countries. Two years later, with a start-up grant from the Bill & Melinda Gates Foundation, Bono cofounded DATA (Debt, AIDS, Trade, Africa), a global advocacy organization for public policy change. Its declared mission was to address poverty, disease, and development in Africa in alliance with government bodies and other multinational NGOs. (Bill Gates would say it was the best million dollars he ever spent.) In 2004, Bono launched the ONE Campaign to catalyze a nonpartisan, grassroots, activist coalition. It's the outside-facing complement to DATA's inside game.

From the time we first met, I was struck by Bono's passion for "factivism," or fact-based activism. In ONE's hardheaded, analytical, results-oriented environment, OKRs were an easy sell. For the last ten years, they've helped clarify the organization's priorities—a tall order when your mission is to change the world. According to David Lane, the organization's former CEO, "We needed a process of discipline to keep us from trying to do everything."

As ONE has grown, it has leaned on OKRs to achieve fundamental culture change. It is pivoting from working *on* Africa to working *in* and *with* Africa. As David told me, "There's been a dramatic philosophical change in how people think about helping the developing world develop itself, to empower these countries to grow on their own. OKRs played a key role in how we did that."

To improve the lives of the world's most vulnerable, ONE has helped deliver nearly $50 billion in funding for historic health initiatives. In addition, it has lobbied successfully for transparency rules to fight corruption, and to channel resources from African oil and gas revenues into the war on extreme poverty. In 2005, alongside Bill and Melinda Gates, Bono was named *Time* magazine's Person of the Year.

———

Bono: We had big goals for U2 from the start. (You could say megalomania set in from a very early age.) Edge was already an accomplished guitar player and Larry was a pretty good drummer, but I was a poor singer and Adam really couldn't play the bass at all. But here's what we thought: We're not as good as those other groups. So we better be *better*.

We weren't as polished or accomplished as the bands we'd go and see, but we had chemistry, whatever the thing is that makes it magic. We thought we could blow up the world if we didn't blow ourselves up first. We felt we could go all the way. The other bands

U2's 360 Tour, 2009.

had everything, but we had *it*. That's what we used to repeat to ourselves.

How did we measure effectiveness? Well, at the outset, we asked questions about our place in the world, beyond the pop charts or the clubs. Like: Can our music be *useful*? Can art inspire political change? In 1979, when we were just eighteen, one of our first jobs was an anti-apartheid show. Another was a pro-contraception show—in Ireland, that was a big deal. Later, in our early twenties, we deliberately became a nuisance to what you might call Irish terror groups and all the people who felt ambivalent about them. We felt compelled to say that blowing up kids in supermarkets can never be right. We gauged our political impact by the torrent of bile that came back at us.

And then at some point, you want your songs to chart. We

worked quite hard to break through to the mainstream, actually. We were a live phenomenon, but our singles didn't do very well. So we judged our success by selling tickets, and then by selling albums.

Picking Our Fights

When we formed our nonprofit DATA, we went about it exactly the same as I had with U2. It was a band: Lucy Matthew, Bobby Shriver, Jamie Drummond, and myself. We didn't know who was the singer or the bass player or the drummer or the guitar player. But we knew we weren't a bunch of hippies and wishful thinkers. We were more punk rock. We were tough-minded opportunists. We were working on a single idea: debt cancellation for the poorest countries. We were good at that, choosing one fight at a time and going at it with a vicious schedule.

Then we went after universal access to anti-AIDS drugs, another clear goal, and I must say, people did laugh in our face: "You are out of your tiny mind. That's impossible. Why fight the most expensive disease when you could have a go at malaria or river blindness? Or finish off polio?"

And I remember saying, "No, we're picking a fight with this disease because these two pills"—it's one pill now—"are a visual representation of inequality. If you live in Dublin or Palo Alto, you can get the pills. If you live in Lilongwe, Malawi, in Africa, you can't get the pills. So because of an accident of longitude and latitude, you live or you die. That doesn't feel right."

Anyway, I was sure we could win that argument, because everyone knew such inequality was wrong. It was that simple. That was years before we used OKRs, but even then I used to say, "Picture

Everest, then describe how difficult the climb is. Then describe how we're going to reach the summit." Like Everest, beating AIDS looked nearly impossible. First you needed to be able to describe it. Then you could climb it.

So now it's 2017, and 21 million people are accessing the antiretroviral therapies. It's amazing. And AIDS-related deaths are down 45 percent in the last ten years. New HIV infections in children are down by more than half. And we're on pace to win the fight against mother-to-child transmission by 2020, to finish the disease off. I believe we will live to see an AIDS-free world in our lifetime.

Growing Up with OKRs

Our NGO band was entrepreneurial in spirit, and we tracked our goals internally. But you can only go so far without process. Once we started to have real impact and real access, DATA merited more data—more measurable procedures, more measurable outcomes. Then we brought eleven different groups together to form a coalition behind the ONE Campaign. We had so many brilliant, gifted people, but our problem was way too many goals. A green revolution in Africa. Girls' education. Energy poverty. Global warming. We were all over the map.

DATA and ONE merged two very different cultures—it was tricky. We realized we were ourselves lacking in transparency. If you don't have clear sign-offs to your goals, you get overlap and dissonance. People get confused about their jobs. For a time we had a real schism in our organization.

Here's the thing: We never thought small. The stretch was always there. But our goals were so gigantic that we stretched too thin and got people worn out. OKRs saved us, really. Tom Freston, chairman of ONE's board, saw their value, so they became part and parcel of the operation—he played a very important role. OKRs forced us to think clearly and agree on what we could achieve with the resources we had. They gave us a frame to hang our passion on. And you need that framework because, without it, your brain is just too abstract. The OKR traffic lights, the color coding—they transformed our board meetings. They sharpened our strategy, our execution, our results. They made us a more effective weapon in the fight against extreme poverty.

The Pivot

When John Doerr arrived at our very first ONE board meeting, he asked a simple and profound question: "Who are we working for? Who's the client here?"

We said, "John, we're working for the world's poorest and most vulnerable." And John said, "Well, then, do they have a seat at the table?"

We said, "Of course, the whole table's there for them."

But John persisted, which was important: "Can you visualize that person? Shouldn't we think about them physically being at this table?"

That's the thinking that seeded the pivot that eventually transformed our organization ONE. John's prodding rhymed with a man we met in Paris once, a man from Senegal. He said, "Bono, do you know the Senegalese proverb 'If you want to cut a man's hair, it is better if he is in the room'?" He said it in a loving way, but we didn't miss the message: *Be careful if you think you know what we want. Because we know what we want. You're not African, and this messiah complex hasn't always turned out so well.*

In 2002, in southeast Africa, I had seen people with HIV queuing up to die. Along with many other AIDS activists, I sent up dramatic flares about the scale and devastation of this pandemic. I encouraged everyone in our organization never to say the word *AIDS* without adding the word *emergency*. "The AIDS emergency." By 2009, though, there was backlash. Some more well-heeled Africans took exception to the way we were characterizing AIDS, though we were right. An economist named Dambisa Moyo wrote a book called *Dead Aid* and led the charge among those who were thinking, "Shove your aid. We don't need it. It's doing more damage than good. We're trying to rebrand the continent as a positive place to invest and live and work. You're hurting that."

I could see that ONE's credibility was under threat here. We had focused on governments in the North because decisions in Washington, London, and Berlin had big consequences for many of the poorest countries. Jamie and other activist friends, like John Githongo, Ory Okolloh, and Rakesh Rajani, were on the ground reminding us of the same thing. Africa's future had to be decided by Africans. We had called our organization ONE, yet we were only half the people necessary to fix these problems. It was fantasy to think those north of the equator could end extreme poverty without a full partnership with those south of the equator.

ONE committed to both organizational and cultural change. Even now, we're still increasing our collaborative work with African leaders—grassroots, grass tops, and all in between. We've established a growing African office in Johannesburg and around the continent. The OKRs have kept us focused on the concrete changes we need to make—hiring staff in Africa, expanding our board, reconnecting with old Jubilee partners, and identifying new networks to turn to for advice. I guess we've become better listeners. And I don't think we could have done it without objectives and key results.

> ## OBJECTIVE
> Proactively integrate a broad range of African perspectives into ONE's work, align more closely with African priorities, and share and leverage ONE's political capital to achieve specific policy changes in and toward Africa.
>
> ### KEY RESULTS
> 1. Three African-based hires complete and onboard by April, and two African board members approved by July.
> 2. African Advisory Board in place by July and convened twice by December.
> 3. Relationships fully developed with a minimum of ten to fifteen leading African thinkers who actively and regularly challenge and guide ONE's policy positions and external work.
> 4. Undertake four participatory trips to Africa over the course of 2010.

Measuring Passion

Having Sudanese businessman and philanthropist Mo Ibrahim on our board is just transformative. In Africa, he is the real deal, a proper rock star. He and his daughter, Hadeel, give us the intellectual static on the continent that we were missing—and that was so necessary to tune in to stronger channels. Before we met him, Mo was properly rude about some of our objectives. He steered us to transparency as a central goal—not just in Africa, but in Europe and America. We put in the research and found that corruption drains a trillion dollars a year from developing countries. "This is more important than HIV/AIDS," Mo told us. "This will save more lives."

With the impetus coming from Africans, ONE's change has progressed. We lobbied side by side with the Publish What You Pay collective, and now it is illegal for any company on the New York Stock Exchange or in the EU to conceal what they've paid for mining rights. And last year, Aliko Dangote, whom I've heard dubbed the Bill Gates of Africa, joined the board.

That's all well and good, but we've also got to be straight about the facts. For example: As of December 2017, ONE has 8.9 million members who have signed up online or have taken part in at least one action. (Over three million of them are now in Africa.) And I can see Bill Gates rolling his eyes and saying, "Big deal. Signers are not members. They're just people who sign something." He's correct, of course. But that led us to a question: How do we measure membership engagement? And whatever metric we come up with, is the number static or can it grow? We needed to prove that we could take people from signers to members to activists to catalysts, so we found ways to thank and reward our members for doing more than one action. We flooded the districts of certain U.S. senators and congresspeople, and it became unnerving for them. For example, if you ask Kay Granger, a Republican congresswoman from Texas, she probably thinks there are people in ONE T-shirts everywhere, pressing her to take a stand. But we're not everywhere; she was one of our strategic targets. And she really came through for ONE.

Bono brings the ONE Campaign to Dalori, Nigeria,
to visit internally displaced persons camps, 2016.

Nobody has ever before measured activists' passion. It sounds odd, but it's totally OKR. So you're passionate—*how* passionate? What actions does your passion lead you to do? And now when Bill Gates asks tough questions at our board meeting, we can bring out our OKRs and say, "Here is what we've done, and this is the impact it's had."

An OKR Framework

Is there a downside to OKRs? Well, if you read them incorrectly, I suppose you could get *too* organized. ONE mustn't get institutional;

we need to stay disruptive. I'm always scared that we're going to go corporate and try to beat every quarterly goal. We needed John to remind us, "If everything's at green, you failed." That was counterintuitive for a lot of people, especially now that we're financed up and have the best and the brightest working here. But John kept saying, "More red!" He was right. We needed more big ambitions because that's what we're good at. We're less good at the incremental stuff.

ONE isn't standing on our passion. We're not standing on our moral outrage. We're standing on a foundation built on certain principles, and with walls and floors—with a certain structure of thinking from the OKRs. And for that, we are very, very grateful. It takes intellectual rigor to effect change; it requires very serious strategies, indeed. If the heart doesn't find a perfect rhyme with the head, then your passion means nothing. The OKR framework cultivates the madness, the chemistry contained inside it. It gives us an environment for risk, for trust, where failing is not a fireable offense—you know, a safe place to be yourself. And when you have that sort of structure and environment, and the right people, magic is around the corner.

And so: Edge was a really talented guitar player from the start, but I wasn't the best singer. Adam wasn't the best bass player. And Larry was just getting there as a drummer. But we had our goals, and a rough idea of how to reach them. We wanted to be the best band in the world.

21

The Goals to Come

What keeps me going is goals.

—*Muhammad Ali*

Ideas are easy; execution is everything.

If you have read this far, you've seen how OKRs and CFRs help organizations of all stripes and sizes move mountains. You've heard firsthand accounts of how they inspire workers, develop leaders, and unify teams to do great things. By measuring what matters, objectives and key results are helping Bono and the Gates Foundation mobilize against poverty and disease in Africa. They're driving Google in its audacious 10x quest to make the world's information freely accessible to all. They're empowering the pizza savants at Zume to deliver a robotically assembled artisanal pie, hot and fresh, to your door.

And here's what's exciting: I think we're just getting started.

OKRs may be called a tool, or a protocol, or a process. But my image of choice is a launch pad, a point of liftoff for the next wave of entrepreneurs and intrapreneurs. My dream is to see Andy Grove's brainchild transform every walk of life. I believe it can have a huge impact on GDP growth, health care outcomes, school success, government performance, business results, and social progress. We're getting glimpses of that future through forward thinkers like Orly Friedman, who has introduced OKRs to every elementary schoolchild at the Khan Lab School in Mountain View, California. (Imagine you are five or six years old and setting your own goals for learning—your own objectives and key results!—as you learn to reason and read.)

I'm convinced that if structured goal setting and continuous communication were to be widely deployed, with rigor and imagination, we could see exponentially greater productivity and innovation throughout society.

OKRs have such enormous potential because they are so adaptable. There is no dogma, no one right way to use them. Different organizations have fluctuating needs at various phases of their life cycle. For some, the simple act of making goals open and transparent is a big leap forward. For others, a quarterly planning cadence will change the game. It's up to you to find your points of emphasis and to make the tool your own.

This book tells a handful of behind-the-scenes stories of OKRs and CFRs. Thousands more are just getting started or have yet to be told. Moving forward, we're going to continue this conversation at whatmatters.com. Come see us there. And you can join the discussion by emailing me at john@whatmatters.com.

My ultimate stretch OKR is to empower people to achieve the seemingly impossible together. To create durable cultures for success *and* significance. And to prime the pump of inspiration for all the goals—especially your goals—that matter most.

DEDICATION

This book is dedicated to two extraordinary people who left us, too soon, within a span of four weeks in 2016. Andy Grove, the brilliant originator of the OKR, is remembered in fair detail in these pages. "Coach" Bill Campbell's wisdom is invoked more fleetingly. Here, then, is our opportunity to celebrate Bill, a man who gave so much to so many. From his gift for honest, open communication to his zeal for data-driven operating excellence, the Coach embodied the very spirit of OKRs. So it's only fitting that he graces our close.

On that clear April morning in Atherton, California, it took a big tent to hold Bill's funeral mass on the Sacred Heart playing fields, the place he'd spent so many Saturdays coaching eighth-graders in flag football or softball. More than three thousand mourners turned out, from Larry Page and Jeff Bezos to generations of the (once) young people who'd played for him. Bill had embraced every one of us with his unabashed bear hugs and self-less guidance. And every one of us believed that Bill was our best friend. His life was the biggest tent of all.

The son of a gym teacher who worked nights at the steel mill in Homestead, Pennsylvania, Bill first earned his sobriquet in the 1970s as varsity football coach at his adored alma mater, Columbia University.* But Coach became *the Coach* when he traded the gridiron for an even more competitive arena, namely the boardrooms and executive suites of Silicon Valley. He was a world-class listener, a hall-of-fame mentor, and the wisest man I've ever met. His ambitious, caring, accountable, transparent, profane humanity built the culture at Google—and dozens of other companies—to what it is today.

As Ken Auletta wrote in *The New Yorker*, "In the world capital of engineering, where per-capita income can seem inversely related to social skills, Campbell was the man who taught founders to look up from their computer screens. . . . His obituary was not featured on the front of most newspapers, or at the top of most technology news sites, but it should have been."

———

We first met in the late eighties. I was recruiting a CEO for one of my most famous failed ventures, the GO Corporation, a pen-based tablet computer company. (Bill's joke was that we should have called it "GO, Going, Gone.") He came recommended by Debra Radabaugh, the top executive recruiter in Silicon Valley, and by his old marketing boss at Apple, Floyd Kvamme, whom I'd recruited to Kleiner Perkins. The deal was sealed when I visited Bill's team at Claris, the Apple software subsidiary. I'm usually quick to judge whether I'm ready to get into trouble with an entrepreneur, though it may take a while longer to persuade them to get into trouble with me. Claris had such great esprit de corps, and such obvious esteem for Bill, that I was sold on the spot.

When Apple and John Sculley refused to spin off Claris in an IPO, as Bill believed had been promised, he took the job at GO. Though our business model flopped, we had a fabulous time to-

---

* Bill had captained the team to its only Ivy League title, in 1961, as a tough-as-nails, 165-pound linebacker. Half a century later, he chaired the university's board of trustees.

*Bill Campbell with his signature beverage for
executive coaching sessions, 2010.*

gether. Before Bill, GO's executive team would preface every vote
with a heated argument over strategy, making for winners, losers,
and general hard feelings. After Bill became CEO, all of that
changed. He'd sit with individual executives and ask them about
their families, and tell a story or two in his colloquial way, and
gradually he'd learn how they felt about the issue at hand. He
had a remarkable way of getting people to agree in advance before they came into the room, and soon there was no more voting at GO. For Bill, it was always about the team, the company.
He was devoid of private motives or agendas. The mission was
paramount.

Bill was a master leader who developed great leaders. Five of
his direct reports at GO became CEOs or CBOs of their own ven-

tures. (I backed every one of them, and every one of them turned a profit.) Among many lessons, Bill taught us the importance of a team's dignity, especially when a company fails. After GO sold out to AT&T, we made sure that those who were let go had great references and found good homes for their careers.

In 1994, I brought Bill back with me to Kleiner Perkins as an "executive in residence," installed him in the corner office next to mine, and promised to find another company for him to run. Around the same time, Intuit founder Scott Cook decided to hire a CEO. Once I introduced Bill to Scott, it took them one walk around Bill's neighborhood in Palo Alto for the Coach to get the job. He and Scott built a tremendous relationship and a spectacular company.

Early in Bill's four-year Intuit tenure, he faced a crisis. Revenues were lagging to the point where they were going to miss the quarter. We had a blue-sky, visionary board of directors that was pushing to invest more capital and power through the shortfall. When the board met in a hotel suite in Las Vegas, the Coach wasn't buying it. "Cut the crap," he said. "We're going to cut back and lay some people off. We're going to get leaner because we've got to make the numbers. It's part of the discipline and the culture I want." Bill felt strongly about delivering results—for the shareholders, but also for the team and the customers.

As we polled the room, however, more and more directors came out for spending and plowing through. Bill looked more and more distraught. When it came around to me, I said, "You know, I think we should go with the Coach." I wasn't sure if he was right or wrong, but I thought it was rightfully his call. My position turned the tide. Later, Bill told me how much what I'd said had meant to him, and that he might have resigned had it gone the other way.

From that point on, we had an unbreakable bond. We could disagree and say some pretty harsh things, but the next day one or the other would call to apologize. Both of us understood that our loyalty—to the relationship, to the team—outweighed any differences.

Bill was still at Intuit when I recruited him for the board at Netscape. Soon he was my first call whenever I backed a new entrepreneur. It became our MO: Kleiner invests, Doerr sponsors, Doerr calls Campbell, Campbell coaches the team. We ran that game plan again and again.

In 1997, Steve Jobs returned to Apple in the most amazing nonhostile takeover of a public company ever, without putting up a penny. Steve asked for the resignations of all but one of Apple's directors, and then he called Bill Campbell to join his new board. The Coach refused to be paid for this work; he was giving back to the Valley that had done so much for him. When a few companies prevailed upon him to accept stock, he funneled the proceeds into his philanthropic organization.

In 2001, after helping persuade Google's founders to hire Eric Schmidt as CEO, I advised Eric that he needed Bill as his coach. Eric was a rightfully proud man who'd already served as CEO and chairman at Novell, and my suggestion offended him—"I know what I'm doing," he said. So it wasn't love at first sight for him and Bill. But in less than a year, Eric's self-review showed how far he'd come around: "Bill Campbell has been very helpful in coaching all of us. In hindsight, his role was needed from the beginning. I should have encouraged this structure sooner, ideally the moment I started at Google."

Bill considered his Google mandate open-ended. He coached Larry Page and Sergey Brin—and Susan Wojcicki and Sheryl Sandberg and Jonathan Rosenberg and Google's whole executive team. He did it in his characteristic style, one part Zen and one part Bud Light. Bill gave little direction. He'd ask a very few questions, invariably the right ones. But mostly he listened. He knew that most times in business there were several right answers, and the leader's job was to pick one. "Just make a decision," he'd say. Or: "Are you moving forward? Are you breaking ties? Let's keep rolling."

When it came to Google's OKRs, Bill paid closest attention to the less glamorous, "committed" objectives. (A favorite piece of coaching, served with his typical dash of salt: "You've got to make the f—ing trains run on time.") As Google CEO Sundar Pichai recalls, "He cared about operating excellence day in, day out." It went back to Bill's deceptively modest-sounding motto: "Be better every day." There is nothing more challenging—or more fulfilling—than that.

The Coach was the éminence grise at Google's Monday executive staff meetings—our unofficial chairman of the board, if you want to know the truth. At the same time, he served as lead outside director on Apple's board, which for anyone else might have presented a conflict. It drove Steve Jobs crazy, especially after Android emerged to challenge the iPhone. Steve harangued Bill forever to choose Apple and leave Google, but the Coach refused: "Steve, I'm not helping Google with their technology. I can't even spell HTML. I'm just helping them be a better business every day." When Steve persisted, the Coach said, "Don't make me choose. You are not going to like the choice I'm going to make." And Steve backed down because the Coach was his one true confidant. (He "kept Steve Jobs going," as Eric Schmidt told *Forbes*. Bill was Steve's "mentor, his friend. He was the protector, the inspiration. Steve trusted him more than he trusted anybody else.")

Though the Coach knew more about technology than he let on, he'd never big-foot engineers or product developers. His superb insights were about leadership, about what made business teams and people tick—and how to protect your people from getting steamrolled by your process. If he saw someone treated unfairly, he'd pick up the phone and call the CEO and say, "This was a process error." And he'd fix it.

People are discouraged from bringing love into business settings, but love was Bill's most distinguishing trait. I can still picture everybody's face lighting up when he'd walk into a meeting at Intuit. Sometimes it was love by faux insult. (If you came to work in an ugly sweater, he'd ask, "Did you roll some guy in the restroom to get that thing?") But you always knew the Coach cared. You always knew he had your back. You always knew he was there for the team. You don't find many leaders who can convey love and fearless feedback at the same time. Bill Campbell was a tough coach, but he was always a players' coach.

More than most in our circles, he *got* family. He was absolutely the happiest when out coaching his daughter Maggie (and my daughter Mary) in softball. He'd be on the field at 3:20 sharp, no matter what big meeting was starting someplace else. And you'd never find the Coach distractedly checking his cell phone in the sixth inning. He was completely present. He sparkled in that setting.

Even after he got sick, Bill never stopped coaching. When I decided to take on the chairmanship of Kleiner Perkins, his advice was a big factor. With my two daughters off to college, the time was right. The Coach knew I wouldn't be slowing down or moving "upstairs." I'd take the job to accelerate what I loved doing: finding and funding the best entrepreneurs, and helping them build great teams as they scaled. It was my chance to become a player-coach for the next generation of leaders and partners. To follow Bill's lead.

A few months before he died, in a podcast with my Kleiner partner Randy Komisar, the Coach explained that he "always wanted to be part of the solution. . . . People are the most important thing that we do. We have to try to make them better."

Bill is gone, but for his many hundreds of disciples, all the executives he coached over all those years, his work goes on. We're still trying to get better every day.

I miss you, Coach. We all do.

John Doerr

April 2018

Coach Bill Campbell, 2013.

RESOURCE 1

Google's OKR Playbook

No one has more collective experience in implementing OKRs than Google. As the company has scaled (and scaled), it has periodically issued OKR guidelines and templates. The following excerpts are drawn mostly from internal sources and reprinted with Google's permission. (Note: This is Google's approach to OKRs. Your approach may—and should—differ.)

————

At Google, we like to think big. We use a process called objectives and key results (OKRs) to help us communicate, measure, and achieve those lofty goals.

Our actions determine Google's future. As we've seen repeatedly—in Search, in Chrome, in Android—a team composed of a few percent of the company's workforce, acting in concert toward an ambitious common goal, can change an entire mature industry in less than two years. Thus it is crucial that as Google employees and managers we make conscious, careful, and informed choices about how we allocate our time and energy—as individuals and as members of teams. OKRs are the manifestation of those careful choices, and the means by which we coordinate the actions of individuals to achieve great collective goals.

We use OKRs to plan what people are going to produce, track their progress vs. plan, and coordinate priorities and milestones between people and teams. We also use OKRs to help people stay focused on the most important goals, and help them avoid being distracted by urgent but less important goals.

OKRs are big, not incremental—we don't expect to hit all of

them. (If we do, we're not setting them aggressively enough.) We grade them with a color scale to measure how well we did:

0.0–0.3 is red

0.4–0.6 is yellow

0.7–1.0 is green

Writing Effective OKRs

Poorly done/managed OKRs are a waste of time, an empty management gesture. Well done OKRs are a motivational management tool that helps make it clear to teams what's important, what to optimize, and what tradeoffs to make during their day-to-day work.

Writing good OKRs isn't easy, but it's not impossible, either. Pay attention to the following simple rules:

Objectives are the "Whats." They:

- express goals and intents;

- are aggressive yet realistic;

- must be tangible, objective, and unambiguous; should be obvious to a rational observer whether an objective has been achieved.

- The successful achievement of an objective must provide clear value for Google.

Key Results are the "Hows." They:

- express measurable milestones which, if achieved, will advance objective(s) in a useful manner to their constituents;

- must describe outcomes, not activities. If your KRs include words like "consult," "help," "analyze," or "participate," they describe activities. Instead, describe the end-user impact of these activities: "publish average and tail latency measurements from six Colossus cells by March 7," rather than "assess Colossus latency";

- must include evidence of completion. This evidence must be available, credible, and easily discoverable. Examples of evidence include change lists, links to docs, notes, and published metrics reports.

Cross-team OKRs

Many important projects at Google require contribution from different groups. OKRs are ideally suited to commit to this coordination. Cross-team OKRs should include all the groups who must materially participate in the OKR, and OKRs committing to each group's contribution should appear explicitly in each such group's OKRs. For example, if Ads Development and Ads SRE and Network Deployment must deliver to support a new ads service, then all three teams should have OKRs describing their commitment to deliver their part of the project.

Committed vs. Aspirational OKRs

OKRs have two variants, and it is important to differentiate between them:

Commitments are OKRs that we agree will be achieved, and we will be willing to adjust schedules and resources to ensure that they are delivered.

- The expected score for a committed OKR is 1.0; a score of less than 1.0 requires explanation for the miss, as it shows errors in planning and/or execution.

By contrast, aspirational OKRs express how we'd like the world to look, even though we have no clear idea how to get there and/or the resources necessary to deliver the OKR.

- Aspirational OKRs have an expected average score of 0.7, with high variance.

Classic OKR-Writing Mistakes and Traps

TRAP #1: Failing to differentiate between committed and aspirational OKRs.
- Marking a committed OKR as aspirational increases the chance of failure. Teams may not take it seriously and may not change their other priorities to focus on delivering the OKR.

- On the other hand, marking an aspirational OKR as committed creates defensiveness in teams who cannot find a way to deliver the OKR, and it invites priority inversion as committed OKRs are de-staffed to focus on the aspirational OKR.

TRAP #2: Business-as-usual OKRs.

- OKRs are often written principally based on what the team believes it can achieve without changing anything they're currently doing, as opposed to what the team or its customers really want.

TRAP #3: Timid aspirational OKRs.

- Aspirational OKRs very often start from the current state and effectively ask, "What could we do if we had extra staff and got a bit lucky?" An alternative and better approach is to start with, "What could my [or my customers'] world look like in several years if we were freed from most constraints?" By definition, you're not going to know how to achieve this state when the OKR is first formulated—that is why it is an aspirational OKR. But without understanding and articulating the desired end state, you guarantee that you are not going to be able to achieve it.

- The litmus test: If you ask your customers what they really want, does your aspirational objective meet or exceed their request?

TRAP #4: Sandbagging.

- A team's committed OKRs should credibly consume most but not all of their available resources. Their committed + aspirational OKRs should credibly consume somewhat more than their available resources. (Otherwise they're effectively commits.)

- Teams who can meet all of their OKRs without needing all of their team's headcount/capital . . . are assumed to either be hoarding resources or not pushing their teams, or both. This is a cue for senior management to reassign headcount and other resources to groups who will make more effective use of them.

TRAP #5: Low Value Objectives (aka the "Who cares?" OKR). OKRs must promise clear business value—otherwise, there's no reason to expend resources doing them. Low Value Objectives (LVOs) are those for which, even if the Objective is completed with a 1.0, no one will notice or care.

- A classic (and seductive) LVO example: "Increase task CPU utilization by 3 percent." This objective by itself does not help users or Google directly. However, the (presumably related) goal, "Decrease quantity of cores required to serve peak queries by 3 percent with no change to quality/latency/ . . . and return resulting excess cores to the free pool" has clear economic value. That's a superior objective.

- Here is a litmus test: Could the OKR get a 1.0 under reasonable circumstances without providing direct end-user or economic benefit? If so, then reword the OKR to focus on the tangible benefit. A classic example: "Launch X," with no criteria for success. Better: "Double fleet-wide Y by launching X to 90+ percent of borg cells."

TRAP #6: Insufficient KRs for committed Os.
- OKRs are divided into the desired outcome (the objective) and the measurable steps required to

achieve that outcome (the key results). It is critical that KRs are written such that scoring 1.0 on all key results generates a 1.0 score for the objective.

- A common error is writing key results that are *necessary but not sufficient* to collectively complete the objective. The error is tempting because it allows a team to avoid the difficult (resource/priority/risk) commitments needed to deliver "hard" key results.

- This trap is particularly pernicious because it delays both the discovery of the resource requirements for the objective, and the discovery that the objective will not be completed on schedule.

- The litmus test: Is it reasonably possible to score 1.0 on all the key results but still not achieve the intent of the objective? If so, add or rework the key results until their successful completion guarantees that the objective is also successfully completed.

Reading, Interpreting, and Acting on OKRs

For committed OKRs
- Teams are expected to rearrange their other priorities to ensure an on-schedule 1.0 delivery.

- Teams who cannot credibly promise to deliver a 1.0 on a committed OKR must escalate promptly. *This is a key point*: Escalating in this (common) situation is not only OK, it is required. Whether the issue arose because of disagreement about the OKR, disagreement about its priority, or inability to allocate enough time/people/resources, escalation is good. It allows the team's management to develop options and resolve conflicts.

  The corollary is that every new OKR is likely to involve some amount of escalation, since it requires a change to existing priorities and commitments. An OKR that requires no changes to any group's activities is a business-as-usual OKR, and those are unlikely to be new—although they may not have previously been written down.

- A committed OKR that fails to achieve a 1.0 by its due date requires a postmortem. This is not intended to punish teams. It is intended to understand what occurred in the planning and/or execution of the OKR, so that teams may improve their ability to reliably hit 1.0 on committed OKRs.

- Examples of classes of committed OKRs are ensuring that a service meets its SLA (service level agreement) for the quarter; or delivering a defined feature or improvement to an infrastructure system by a set date; or manufacturing and delivering a quantity of servers at a cost point.

Aspirational OKRs

- The set of aspirational OKRs will by design exceed the team's ability to execute in a given quarter. The OKRs' priority should inform team members' decisions on where to spend the remaining time they have after the group's commitments are met. In general, higher priority OKRs should be completed before lower priority OKRs.

- Aspirational OKRs and their associated priorities should remain on a team's OKR list until they are completed, carrying them forward from quarter to quarter as necessary. Dropping them from the OKR list because of lack of progress is a mistake, as it disguises persistent problems of prioritization, resource availability, or a lack of understanding of the problem/solution.

  Corollary: It is good to move an aspirational OKR to a different team's list if that team has both the expertise and bandwidth to accomplish the OKR more effectively than the current OKR owner.

- Team managers are expected to assess the resources required to accomplish their aspirational OKRs and *ask for them* each quarter, fulfilling their duty to express known demand to the business. Managers should not expect to receive all the required resources, however, unless their aspirational OKRs are the highest priority goals in the company after the committed OKRs.

More Litmus Tests

Some simple tests to see if your OKRs are good:

- If you wrote them down in five minutes, they probably aren't good. Think.

- If your objective doesn't fit on one line, it probably isn't crisp enough.

- If your KRs are expressed in team-internal terms ("Launch Foo 4.1"), they probably aren't good. What matters isn't the launch, but its impact. Why is Foo 4.1 important? Better: "Launch Foo 4.1 to improve sign-ups by 25 percent." Or simply: "Improve sign-ups by 25 percent."

- Use real dates. If every key result happens on the last day of the quarter, you likely don't have a real plan.

- Make sure your key results are measurable: It must be possible to objectively assign a grade at the end of the quarter. "Improve sign-ups" isn't a good key result. Better: "Improve daily sign-ups by 25 percent by May 1."

- Make sure the metrics are unambiguous. If you say "1 million users," is that all-time users or seven-day actives?

- If there are important activities on your team (or a significant fraction of its effort) that aren't covered by OKRs, add more.

- For larger groups, make OKRs hierarchical—have high-level ones for the entire team, more detailed ones for subteams. Make sure that the "horizontal" OKRs (projects that need multiple teams to contribute) have supporting key results in each subteam.

RESOURCE 2

A Typical OKR Cycle

Let's assume you are setting OKRs at the company, team, and contributor levels. (Larger companies may have additional levels.)

4–6 weeks before quarter

Brainstorm Annual and Q1 OKRs for Company
Senior leaders start brainstorming top-line company OKRs. If you're setting OKRs for Q1, this is also the time to set your annual plan, which can help guide the direction of company.

2 weeks before quarter

Communicate Company-wide OKRs for Upcoming Year and Q1
Finalize company OKRs and communicate them to everyone.

Start of quarter

Communicate Team Q1 OKRs
Based on the company's OKRs, teams develop their own OKRs and share them at their meetings.

1 week after Start of quarter

Share Employee Q1 OKRs
One week after team OKRs are communicated, contributors share their own OKRs. This may require negotiation between contributors and their managers, typically in one-on-one settings.

Throughout quarter

Employees Track Progress and Check-in
Throughout the quarter, employees measure and share their progress, checking in regularly with their managers. Periodically through the quarter, contributors assess how likely they are to fully achieve their OKRs. If attainment appears unlikely, they may need to recalibrate.

Near end of quarter

Employees Reflect and Score Q1 OKRs
Toward the end of the quarter, contributors score their OKRs, perform a self-assessment, and reflect on what they have accomplished.

All Talk: Performance Conversations

Continuous performance management is a two-part, interwoven process. The first part consists of setting OKRs; the second entails regular and ongoing conversations, tailored to your needs.

Goal Planning and Reflection

To help facilitate this conversation, a manager might ask a contributor the following:

- What OKRs do you plan to focus on to drive the greatest value for your role, your team, and/or the company?

- Which of these OKRs aligns to key initiatives in the organization?

Progress Updates

To get the contributor talking, a manager might pose these questions:

- How are your OKRs coming along?

- What critical capabilities do you need to be successful?

- Is there anything stopping you from attaining your objectives?

- What OKRs need to be adjusted—or added, or eliminated—in light of shifting priorities?

Manager-led Coaching

To prepare for this conversation, the manager should consider the following questions:

- What behaviors or values do I want my report to continue to exhibit?

- What behaviors or values do I want the report to start or stop exhibiting?

- What coaching can I provide to help the report fully realize his or her potential?

- During the conversation, the leader might ask:

  What part of your job most excites you?

  What (if any) aspect of your role would you like to change?

Upward Feedback

To elicit candid input from a contributor, the manager might ask:

- What are you getting from me that you find helpful?

- What are you getting from me that impedes your ability to be effective?

- What could I do for you that would help you to be more successful?

Career Growth

To tease out a contributor's career aspirations, a manager might ask:

- What skills or capabilities would you like to develop to improve in your current role?

- In what areas do you want to grow to achieve your career goals?

- What skills or capabilities would you like to develop for a future role?

- From a learning, growth, and development standpoint, how can I and the company help you get there?

Prepping for Performance Conversations

Before launching a performance conversation with a contributor, some prep work is in order. Specifically, leaders should consider the following:

- What were the contributor's main objectives and responsibilities in the period in question?

- How has the contributor performed?

- If the contributor is underperforming, how should he or she course-correct?

- If the contributor is performing well or exceeding expectations, what can I do to sustain a high level of performance without burnout?

- When is the contributor most engaged?

- When is the contributor least engaged?

- What strengths does the contributor bring to the work?

- What types of learning experience might benefit this contributor?

- Over the next six months, what should the contributor's focus be? Meeting expectations in his or her current role? Maximizing contributions in the current role? Or preparing for the next opportunity—be it a new project, expanded responsibility, or new role?

Contributors, too, should prepare for performance conversations. Specifically, they can ask themselves:

- Am I on track to meet my objectives?

- Have I identified areas of opportunity?

- Do I understand how my work connects to broader milestones?

- What feedback can I give my manager?

In Sum

Four Superpowers of OKRs
1. **Focus and Commit to Priorities**
2. **Align and Connect for Teamwork**
3. **Track for Accountability**
4. **Stretch for Amazing**

Continuous Performance Management
Importance of Culture

Focus and Commit to Priorities

- Set the appropriate cadence for your OKR cycle. I recommend dual tracking, with quarterly OKRs (for shorter-term goals) and annual OKRs (keyed to longer-term strategies) deployed in parallel.

- To work out implementation kinks and strengthen leaders' commitment, phase in your rollout of OKRs with upper management first. Allow the process to gain momentum before enlisting individual contributors to join in.

- Designate an OKR shepherd to make sure that every individual devotes the time each cycle to choosing what matters most.

- Commit to three to five top objectives—*what* you need to achieve—per cycle. Too many OKRs dilute and scatter people's efforts. Expand your effective capacity by deciding what *not* to do, and discard, defer, or deemphasize accordingly.

- In choosing OKRs, look for objectives with the most leverage for outstanding performance.

- Find the raw material for top-line OKRs in the organization's mission statement, strategic plan, or a broad theme chosen by leadership.

- To emphasize a departmental objective and enlist lateral support, elevate it to a company OKR.

- For each objective, settle on no more than five measurable, unambiguous, time-bound key results—*how* the objective will be attained. By definition, completion of all key results equates to the attainment of the objective.

- For balance and quality control, pair qualitative and quantitative key results.

- When a key result requires extra attention, elevate it into an objective for one or more cycles.

- The single most important element for OKR success is conviction and buy-in by the organization's leaders.

Align and Connect for Teamwork

- Incentivize employees by showing how their objectives relate to the leader's vision and the company's top priorities. The express route to operating excellence is lined with transparent, public goals, on up to the CEO.

- Use all-hands meetings to explain why an OKR is important to the organization. Then keep repeating the message until you're tired of hearing it yourself.

- When deploying cascaded OKRs, with objectives driven from the top, welcome give-and-take on key results from frontline contributors. Innovation dwells less at a company's center than at its edges.

- Encourage a healthy proportion of bottom-up OKRs— roughly half.

- Smash departmental silos by connecting teams with horizontally shared OKRs. Cross-functional operations enable quick and coordinated decisions, the basis for seizing a competitive advantage.

- Make all lateral, cross-functional dependencies explicit.

- When an OKR is revised or dropped, see to it that all stakeholders know about it.

Track for Accountability

- To build a culture of accountability, install continuous reassessment and honest and objective grading—and start at the top. When leaders openly admit their missteps, contributors feel freer to take healthy risks.

- Motivate contributors less with extrinsic rewards and more with open, tangible measures of their achievement.

- To keep OKRs timely and relevant, have the designated shepherd ride herd over regular check-ins and progress updates. Frequent check-ins enable teams and individuals to course-correct with agility, or to fail fast.

- To sustain high performance, encourage weekly one-on-one OKR meetings between contributors and managers, plus monthly departmental meetings.

- As conditions change, feel free to revise, add, or delete OKRs as appropriate—even in mid-cycle. Goals are not written in stone. It's counterproductive to hold stubbornly to objectives that are no longer relevant or attainable.

- At the cycle's end, use OKR grades plus subjective self-assessments to evaluate past performance, celebrate achievements, and plan and improve for the future.

Before pushing into the next cycle, take a moment to reflect upon and savor what you've accomplished in the last one.

- To keep OKRs up-to-date and on point, invest in a dedicated, automated, cloud-based platform. Public, collaborative, real-time goal-setting systems work best.

Stretch for Amazing

- At the beginning of each cycle, distinguish between goals that must be attained 100 percent (committed OKRs) and those that are stretching for a Big Hairy Audacious Goal (a BHAG, or aspirational OKR).

- Establish an environment where individuals are free to fail without judgment.

- To stimulate problem solving and spur people to greater achievement, set ambitious goals—even if it means some quarterly targets will be missed. But don't set the bar so high that an OKR is obviously unrealistic. Morale suffers when people know they can't succeed.

- To get leaps in productivity or innovation, follow Google's "Gospel of 10x" and replace incremental OKRs with exponential ones. That's how industries get disrupted and categories reinvented.

- Design stretch OKRs to fit the organization's culture. A company's optimal "stretch" may vary over time, depending on the operating needs of the coming cycle.

- When a team fails to attain a stretch OKR, consider rolling the objective over to the next cycle—assuming the goal is still relevant.

Continuous Performance Management

- To address issues before they become problems and give struggling contributors the support they need, move from annual performance management to *continuous* performance management.

- Unleash ambitious goal setting by divorcing forward-looking OKRs from backward-looking annual reviews. Equating goal attainment to bonus checks will invite sandbagging and risk-averse behavior.

- Replace competitive ratings and stack rankings with transparent, strength-based, multidimensional criteria for performance evaluations. Beyond the numbers, consider a contributor's team play, communication, and ambition in goal setting.

- Rely on intrinsic motivations—purposeful work and opportunities for growth—over financial incentives. They're far more powerful.

- To power positive business results, implement ongoing CFRs (conversations, feedback, and recognition) in concert with structured goal setting. Transparent OKRs make coaching more concrete and useful. Continuous CFRs keep day-to-day work on point and genuinely collaborative.

- In performance-driving conversations between managers and contributors, allow the contributor to set the agenda. The manager's role is to learn and coach.

- Make performance feedback two-way, ad hoc, and multidirectional, unconstrained by the org chart.

- Use anonymous "pulse" surveys for real-time feedback on particular operations or general morale.

- Strengthen connections between teams and departments with peer-to-peer feedback, in conjunction with cross-functional OKRs.

- Employ peer recognition to enhance employee engagement and performance. For maximum impact, recognition should be frequent, specific, highly visible, and tied to top-line OKRs.

The Importance of Culture

- Align top-line OKRs with an organization's mission, vision, and North Star values.

- Convey cultural values by word, but most of all by deed.

- Promote peak performance with collaboration and accountability. When OKRs are collective, assign key results to individuals—and hold them accountable.

- To develop a high-motivation culture, balance OKR "catalysts," actions that support the work, with CFR "nourishers," acts of interpersonal support or even random acts of kindness.

- Use OKRs to promote transparency, clarity, purpose, and big-picture orientation. Deploy CFRs to build positivity, enthusiasm, stretch thinking, and daily improvement.

- Be alert to the need to address cultural barriers, especially issues of accountability and trust, *before* implementing OKRs.

For Further Reading

Andy Grove and Intel
- *High Output Management*, by Andrew S. Grove

- *Andy Grove: The Life and Times of an American*, by Richard S. Tedlow

- *The Intel Trinity: How Robert Noyce, Gordon Moore, and Andy Grove Built the World's Most Important Company*, by Michael Malone

Culture
- *HOW: Why HOW We Do Anything Means Everything*, by Dov Seidman

- *Lean In: Women, Work, and the Will to Lead*, by Sheryl Sandberg

- *Radical Candor: Be a Kick-Ass Boss Without Losing Your Humanity*, by Kim Scott

Jim Collins
- *Good to Great: Why Some Companies Make the Leap . . . and Others Don't*

- *Great by Choice: Uncertainty, Chaos, and Luck—Why Some Thrive Despite Them All*

Bill Campbell and Coaching

- *Playbook: The Coach—Lessons Learned from Bill Campbell,* forthcoming book by Eric Schmidt, Jonathan Rosenberg, and Alan Eagle

- *Straight Talk for Startups: 100 Insider Rules for Beating the Odds,* by Randy Komisar

Google

- *How Google Works,* by Eric Schmidt and Jonathan Rosenberg

- *Work Rules!: Insights from Inside Google That Will Transform How You Live and Lead,* by Laszlo Bock

- *In the Plex: How Google Thinks, Works, and Shapes Our Lives,* by Steven Levy

OKRs

- www.whatmatters.com

- *Radical Focus: Achieving Your Most Important Goals with Objectives and Key Results,* by Christina Wodtke

ACKNOWLEDGMENTS

I n closing this edition of *Measure What Matters*, I feel an over-whelming sense of gratitude. First, that I was so lucky to be heir to Andy Grove's system to amplify human potential. And then to watch inspiring entrepreneurs, leaders, and teams adapt it to reach for their dreams. I am also thankful for our great country that rewards risk taking, something I never take for granted.

Most of all, I thank you, my readers, for your attention, engagement, and feedback. I hope you'll write to me at john@whatmat ters.com.

The coming-to-be of this book confirms my mantra that it takes a team to win. From inception to finished product, I thank the Portfolio/Penguin team that made it all possible: my publisher, Adrian Zackheim, who foresaw its potential; my superlative editor, Stephanie Frerich, who went so many extra miles and somehow kept her good humor; and also Tara Gilbride, Olivia Peluso, and Will Weisser. I am grateful as well to my agent, Myrsini Stephanides, and my attorney, Peter Moldave. And to the skilled and versatile Ryan Panchadsaram, whose insights and judgment proved indispensable.

A special thank-you goes to the individuals who took time out of their impossibly busy schedules to read the manuscript and offer the feedback that made it so much better:

To Bing Gordon, who also introduced me to Debra Radabaugh, who introduced me to Coach Campbell.

I thank Jonathan Rosenberg, who furnished so many perceptive observations on the Google way of using OKRs and pointed me to our "stretch" case studies.

Thanks to Laszlo Bock, a brilliant thought leader on goals, continuous performance management, and culture. And to Dov Seidman, the great business philosopher, for his wisdom on culture and values.

Thank you Tom Friedman, Laurene Powell Jobs, Al Gore, Randy Komisar and Sheryl Sandberg, friends with big brains and kind hearts, who shared their unique values and wisdom on building teams and institutions.

Thanks to Jim Collins, my favorite business author, whose data-driven, crystalline thinking challenged and clarified my purpose. I couldn't have written this book had Jim not pointed the way forward in his own groundbreaking work.

And I thank Walter Isaacson, biographer extraordinaire, whose good counsel and advice were instrumental as *Measure What Matters* began to take shape.

I'd also like to thank my partners at Kleiner Perkins, whose commitment to entrepreneurs lifts me up every day: Mike Abbott, Brook Byers, Eric Feng, Bing Gordon, Mamoon Hamid, Wen Hsieh, Noah Knauf, Randy Komisar, Mary Meeker, Mood Rowghani, Ted Schlein, and Beth Seidenberg. Also, thanks to Sue Biglieri, Alix Burns, Juliet deBaubigny, Amanda Duckworth, Rouz Jazayeri, and Scott Ryles. And a special thanks to Rae Nell Rhodes, Cindy Chang, and Noelle Miraglia for their unflagging support, and Tina Case, who found the photographs that brought this book to life.

The four OKR superpowers, supported and made meaningful by CFRs, are the scaffolding for *Measure What Matters*. But this book would be hollow without our insider stories to depict OKRs and

Acknowledgments

CFRs in real life and real time. So here is a special thanks to the storytellers, who shared so generously from their experiences.

I want to start with the Gates Foundation team, past and present, who are especially inspiring for the breathtaking scope and lifesaving impact of their work. Thank you, Bill and Melinda, Patty Stonesifer, Larry Cohen, Bridgitt Arnold, Sylvia Mathews Burwell, Susan Desmond-Hellman, Mark Suzman, and Ankur Vora. Your achievement will make its own epic book that we cannot wait to read.

Thanks to our favorite Irish rock star, who has built a global crusade to fight disease, poverty, and corruption. Thank you Bono and your team of Jamie Drummond, David Lane, Lucy Matthew, Bobby Shriver, Gayle Smith, and Ken Weber for your creation of ONE.

Now, the Google gang merits special mention. Yes, Larry Page, Sergey Brin, and Eric Schmidt have made Google the twenty-first-century prototype for structured goal setting. Their resolve and results with OKRs impressed even Andy Grove. But I would be remiss not to recognize as well the 100,000-plus Google employees and alumni who have spread the goals gospel globally. I particularly thank Sundar Pichai, Susan Wojcicki, Jonathan Rosenberg, and Cristos Goodrow. Also, Tim Armstrong, Raja Ayyagari, Shona Brown, Chris Dale, Beth Dowd, Salar Kamangar, Winnie King, Rick Klau, Shishir Mehrotra, Eileen Naughton, Ruth Porat, Brian Rakowski, Prasad Setty, Ram Shriram, Esther Sun, Matt Susskind, Astro Teller, and Kent Walker.

Intel's past and present leaders were magnanimous with their insights. Thank you to Gordon Moore, Les Vadasz, Eva Grove, Bill Davidow, Dane Elliott, Jim Lally, and Casey Powell. Also to CEO Brian Krzanich, Steve Rodgers, Kelly Kelly, and to Terry Murphy, Andy Grove's longtime executive assistant.

From Remind: Brett Kopf, David Kopf, and Brian Grey.

From Nuna: Jini Kim, David Chen, Katja Gussman, Nick Sung, and Sanjey Sivanesan.

From MyFitnessPal: Mike Lee and David Lee.

From Intuit: Atticus Tysen, Scott Cook, Brad Smith, Sherry Whiteley, and Olga Braylovskliy.

From Adobe: Donna Morris, Shantanu Narayen, and Dan Rosensweig.

From Zume: Julia Collins and Alex Garden.

From Coursera: Lila Ibrahim, Daphne Koller, Andrew Ng, Rick Levin, and Jeff Maggioncalda.

From Lumeris: Andrew Cole, Art Glasgow, and Mike Long.

From Schneider Electric: Hervé Coureil and Sharon Abraham.

From Walmart: John Brothers, Becky Schmitt, and Angela Christman.

From Khan Academy: Orly Friedman and Sal Khan.

I am honored to acknowledge the experts who lent their insights, input, and many contributions to the OKR movement and this book: Alex Barnett; Tracy Beltrane; Ethan Bernstein; Josh Bersin; Ben Brookes; John Brothers; Aaron Butkus; Ivy Choy; John Chu; Roger Corn; Angus Davis; Chris Deptula; Patrick Foley; Uwe Higgen; Arnold Hur; General Tom Kolditz; Cory Kreeck; Jonathan Lesser; Aaron Levie; Kevin Louie; Denise Lyle; Chris Mason; Amelia Merrill; Deep Nishar; Bill Pence; Stephanie Pimmel; Philip Potloff; Aurelie Richard; Dr. David Rock; Timo Salzsieder; Jake Schmidt; Erin Sharp; Jeff Smith; Tim Staffa; Joseph Suzuki; Chris Villar; Jeff Weiner; Christina Wodtke; and Jessica Woodall.

Thanks especially to CEO Doug Dennerline and the goal-oriented crew at BetterWorks, who are advancing OKRs and CFRs like no one else while working better themselves every day.

Not least, I'd like to thank some special individuals with whom I've been privileged to work over the years, and whose lives are exemplars of excellence. Notable among them: Jim Barksdale, Andy Bechtolsheim, Jeff Bezos, Scott Cook, John Chambers, Bill Joy, and KR Sridhar. And Andy Grove, Bill Campbell, and Steve Jobs, gone but never to be forgotten.

I sincerely thank Jeff Coplon, who was at the center of the team that made this happen—and who proved, once again, that execution is everything.

Long before I encountered OKRs, my father and hero, Lou Doerr, taught me the value of focus, commitment, high standards, and higher aspirations (and RMA—the Right Mental Attitude). My mother, Rosemary Doerr, gave me her unconditional support to put those lessons into practice.

Finally, I offer my undying gratitude to my wife, Ann, and daughters, Mary and Esther, whose patience, encouragement, and love kept me going through this long and challenging project. Each and every day, they remind me of what matters the most.

NOTES

Chapter 1: Google, Meet OKRs

7 As prize pupil Marissa Mayer: Steven Levy, *In the Plex: How Google Thinks, Works, and Shapes Our Lives* (New York: Simon & Schuster, 2011). In some cases, the key result is binary, either done or not: "Complete onboarding manual for new hires."

8 "Goals Gone Wild": Lisa D. Ordóñez, Maurice E. Schweitzer, Adam D. Galinsky, and Max H. Bazerman, "Goals Gone Wild: The Systematic Side Effects of Overprescribing Goal Setting," *Academy of Management Perspectives*, February 1, 2009.

9 "Goals may cause": Ibid.

9 said Edwin Locke, "hard goals": Edwin Locke, "Toward a Theory of Task Motivation and Incentives," *Organizational Behavior and Human Performance*, May 1968.

9 "one of the most tested": "The Quantified Serf," *The Economist*, March 7, 2015.

10 "involved in, enthusiastic about": Annamarie Mann and Jim Harter, "The Worldwide Employee Engagement Crisis," gallup.com, January 7, 2016. Worldwide, only 13 percent of employees are engaged. Moreover, according to Deloitte, it's not getting better; engagement levels are no higher today than they were ten years ago.

10 In the technology sector: Dice Tech Salary Survey, 2014, http://marketing.dice.com/pdf/Dice_TechSalarySurvey_2015.pdf.

10 More highly engaged work groups: Annamarie Mann and Ryan Darby, "Should Managers Focus on Performance or Engagement?" *Gallup Business Journal*, August 5, 2014.

10 "retention and engagement": *Global Human Capital Trends 2014*, Deloitte University Press.

10 "clearly defined goals": "Becoming Irresistible: A New Model for Employee Engagement," *Deloitte Review*, Issue 16, January 26, 2015.

10 **"When people have conflicting priorities":** Teresa Amabile and Steven Kramer, *The Progress Principle: Using Small Wins to Ignite Joy, Engagement, and Creativity at Work* (Boston: Harvard Business Review Press, 2011).

10 **goals "can inspire employees":** Ordóñez, Schweitzer, Galinsky, and Bazerman, "Goals Gone Wild."

11 **As Schmidt told:** Levy, *In the Plex.*

13 **OKRs became the "simple tool":** Eric Schmidt and Jonathan Rosenberg, *How Google Works* (New York: Grand Central Publishing, 2014).

14 **In 2008, a company-wide:** Levy, *In the Plex.*

14 **When Jonathan Rosenberg:** Schmidt and Rosenberg, *How Google Works.*

15 **In 2017, for the sixth:** *Fortune*, March 15, 2017.

CHAPTER 2: The Father of OKRs

22 **In the space:** While there's no record of the session I attended, we unearthed a video recording of a similar seminar Grove gave three years later. The attributed remarks are sourced from that recording and hosted on www.whatmatters.com.

24 **Scientific management, Taylor wrote:** Frederick Winslow Taylor, *The Principles of Scientific Management* (New York and London: Harper & Brothers, 1911).

24 **"crisp and hierarchical":** Andrew S. Grove, *High Output Management* (New York: Random House, 1983).

24 **"a principle of management":** Peter F. Drucker, *The Practice of Management* (New York: Harper & Row, 1954).

25 **In a meta-analysis:** Robert Rodgers and John E. Hunter, "Impact of Management by Objectives on Organizational Productivity," *Journal of the American Psychological Association,* April 1991.

25 **"just another tool":** "Management by Objectives," *The Economist,* October 21, 2009.

26 **He sought to "create":** Grove, *High Output Management.*

26 **Andy recruited "aggressive introverts":** Andrew S. Grove, iOPEC seminar, 1978. For one contemporary example, Larry Page is an aggressive introvert.

30 **As one Intel historian:** Tim Jackson, *Inside Intel: The Story of Andrew Grove and the Rise of the World's Most Powerful Chip Company* (New York: Dutton, 1997).

31 **As he once told:** *New York Times,* December 23, 1980.

32 **"one of the most acclaimed":** *New York Times,* March 21, 2016.

33 **"the person most responsible":** *Time,* December 29, 1997.

CHAPTER 3: Operation Crush: An Intel Story

36 "There's only one company": Tim Jackson, *Inside Intel: The Story of Andrew Grove and the Rise of the World's Most Powerful Chip Company* (New York: Dutton, 1997).

37 Crush veterans recalled: "Intel Crush Oral History Panel," Computer History Museum, October 14, 2013.

CHAPTER 4: Superpower #1: Focus and Commit to Priorities

49 values cannot be transmitted: Andrew S. Grove, *High Output Management* (New York: Random House, 1983).

49 "When you're the CEO": "Lessons from Bill Campbell, Silicon Valley's Secret Executive Coach," podcast with Randy Komisar, soundcloud .com, February 2, 2016, https://soundcloud.com/venturedpodcast/bill _campbell.

50 two of three companies: Stacia Sherman Garr, "High-Impact Performance Management: Using Goals to Focus the 21st-Century Workforce," Bersin by Deloitte, December 2014.

50 In a survey: Donald Sull and Rebecca Homkes, "Why Senior Managers Can't Name Their Firms' Top Priorities," London Business School, December 7, 2015.

50 "must be able to measure": Peter F. Drucker, *The Practice of Management* (New York: Harper & Row, 1954).

51 "For the feedback": Grove, *High Output Management.*

52 "with an iron hand": Mark Dowie, "Pinto Madness," *Mother Jones*, September/October 1977.

52 Safety was nowhere: Ibid. As Iacocca liked to say, "Safety doesn't sell."

53 "The specific, challenging goals": Lisa D. Ordóñez, Maurice E. Schweitzer, Adam D. Galinsky, and Max H. Bazerman, "Goals Gone Wild: The Systematic Side Effects of Overprescribing Goal Setting," Harvard Business School working paper, February 11, 2009, www.hbs.edu/faculty /Publication%20Files/09-083.pdf.

53 a manager's teenage daughter: Stacy Cowley and Jennifer A. Kingson, "Wells Fargo Says 2 Ex-Leaders Owe $75 Million More," *New York Times*, April 11, 2017.

53 "their paired counterparts": Grove, *High Output Management.*

56 "The one thing": Ibid.

57 "The *art* of management": Ibid.

CHAPTER 5: Focus: The Remind Story

58 **Class participation rose:** Matthew Kraft, "The Effect of Teacher-Family Communication on Student Engagement: Evidence from a Randomized Field Experiment," *Journal of Research on Educational Effectiveness*, June 2013.

CHAPTER 6: Commit: The Nuna Story

76 **Andrew M. Slavitt:** Steve Lohr, "Medicaid's Data Gets an Internet-Era Makeover," *New York Times*, January 9, 2017.

CHAPTER 7: Superpower #2: Align and Connect for Teamwork

77 **Research shows that public:** Based on BetterWorks' analysis of 100,000 goals.

77 **In a recent survey:** Wakefield Research, November 2016.

79 **The term for this linkage:** According to the *Harvard Business Review*, companies with highly aligned employees are more than twice as likely to be top performers as their competition ("How Employee Alignment Boosts the Bottom Line," *Harvard Business Review*, June 16, 2016).

79 **Studies suggest that:** Robert S. Kaplan and David P. Norton, *The Strategy-Focused Organization: How Balanced Scorecard Companies Thrive in the New Business Environment* (Boston: Harvard Business School Press, 2001).

79 **a poll of global CEOs:** Donald Sull, "Closing the Gap Between Strategy and Execution," *MIT Sloan Management Review*, July 1, 2007.

79 **"We've got a lot":** Interview with Amelia Merrill, people strategy leader at RMS.

86 **"Having goals improves performance":** Laszlo Bock, *Work Rules!: Insights from Inside Google That Will Transform How You Live and Lead* (New York: Grand Central Publishing, 2015).

87 **"People in the trenches":** Andrew S. Grove, *Only the Paranoid Survive: How to Identify and Exploit the Crisis Points That Challenge Every Business* (New York: Doubleday Business, 1996).

87 **The "professional employee":** Peter Drucker, *The Practice of Management* (New York: Harper & Row, 1954).

87 **dim view of "managerial meddling":** Andrew S. Grove, *High Output Management* (New York: Random House, 1983).

88 **"The higher the goals":** Edwin Locke and Gary Latham, "Building a Practically Useful Theory of Goal Setting and Task Motivation: A 35-Year Odyssey," *American Psychologist*, September 2002.

89 **"People across the whole":** Interview with Laszlo Bock, former head of Google's People Operations.

Chapter 9: Connect: The Intuit Story

102 **for fourteen years running:** http://beta.fortune.com/worlds-most-ad mired-companies/intuit-100000.

102 **"Whenever Intuit makes":** Vindu Goel, "Intel Sheds Its PC Roots and Rises as a Cloud Software Company," *New York Times*, April 10, 2016.

Chapter 10: Superpower #3: Track for Accountability

117 **Research suggests that making:** Teresa Amabile and Steven Kramer, *The Progress Principle: Using Small Wins to Ignite Joy, Engagement, and Creativity at Work* (Boston: Harvard Business Review Press, 2011).

117 **"The single greatest motivator":** Daniel H. Pink, *Drive: The Surprising Truth About What Motivates Us* (New York: Riverhead Books, 2009).

117 **"Without an action plan":** Peter Drucker, *The Effective Executive: The Definitive Guide to Getting the Right Things Done* (New York: Harper & Row, 1967).

117 **In one California study:** Research by Gail Matthews, Dominican University of California, www.dominican.edu/dominicannews/study-highlights -strategies-for-achieving-goals.

119 **"If the ladder is not":** Stephen R. Covey, *The 7 Habits of Highly Effective People* (New York: Simon & Schuster, 1989).

119 **"people can learn from failure":** "Don't Be Modest: Decrypting Google," *The Economist*, September 27, 2014.

125 **Learning "from direct experience":** Giada Di Stefano, Francesca Gino, Gary Pisano, and Bradley Staats, "Learning by Thinking: How Reflection Improves Performance," Harvard Business School working paper, April 11, 2014.

125 **"We do not learn":** Ibid.

Chapter 12: Superpower #4: Stretch for Amazing

133 **For companies seeking:** Steve Kerr, "Stretch Goals: The Dark Side of Asking for Miracles," *Fortune*, November 13, 1995.

133 **As Bill Campbell liked:** Podcast with Randy Komisar, soundcloud.com, February 2, 2016.

133 **"A BHAG is a huge":** Jim Collins, *Good to Great: Why Some Companies Make the Leap . . . and Others Don't* (New York: HarperCollins, 2001).

134 **the results were "unequivocal":** Edwin A. Locke, "Toward a Theory of Task Motivation and Incentives," *Organizational Behavior and Human Performance* 3, 1968.

134 **"Setting specific challenging goals"**: Edwin A. Locke and Gary P. Latham, "Building a Practically Useful Theory of Goal Setting and Task Motivation: A 35-Year Odyssey," *American Psychologist*, September 2002.

137 **"stretched" goals could elicit**: Andrew S. Grove, *High Output Management* (New York: Random House, 1983).

137 **"This is Intel"**: "Intel Crush Oral History Panel," Computer History Museum, October 14, 2013.

138 **By the third quarter**: William H. Davidow, *Marketing High Technology: An Insider's View* (New York: Free Press, 1986).

138 **"the gospel of 10x"**: Steven Levy, "Big Ideas: Google's Larry Page and the Gospel of 10x," *Wired*, March 30, 2013.

139 **"tend to assume that"**: Eric Schmidt and Jonathan Rosenberg, *How Google Works* (New York: Grand Central Publishing, 2014).

139 **"The way Page sees it"**: Levy, "Big Ideas."

140 **start of the period**: Interview with Bock.

141 **In pursuing high-effort**: Locke and Latham, "Building a Practically Useful Theory of Goal Setting and Task Motivation."

142 **"You know, in our business"**: iOPEC seminar, 1992.

CHAPTER 13: Stretch: The Google Chrome Story

143 **"If you want your car"**: Laszlo Bock, *Work Rules!: Insights from Inside Google That Will Transform How You Live and Lead* (New York: Grand Central Publishing, 2015).

143 **"If you set a crazy"**: Ibid.

150 **"Dear Sophie," a spot**: https://whatmatters.com/sophie.

CHAPTER 14: Stretch: The YouTube Story

154 **"the most powerful woman"**: Belinda Luscombe, "Meet YouTube's Viewmaster," *Time*, August 27, 2015.

161 **"the true scarce commodity"**: Satya Nadella, company-wide email to Microsoft employees, June 25, 2015.

CHAPTER 15: Continuous Performance Management: OKRs and CFRs

176 **Yet only 12 percent**: "Performance Management: The Secret Ingredient," Deloitte University Press, February 27, 2015.

176 **Only 6 percent think**: "Global Human Capital Trends 2014: Engaging the 21st Century Workforce," Bersin by Deloitte.

176 **A manager's "first role"**: www.druckerinstitute.com/2013/07/measurement-myopia.

179 **Table 15.1: Annual Performance Management:** Josh Bersin and Better-Works, "How Goals Are Driving a New Approach to Performance Management," Human Capital Institute, April 4, 2016.

182 **Andy Grove estimated:** Andrew S. Grove, *High Output Management* (New York: Random House, 1983).

183n **Andy believed the "subordinate":** "Former Intel CEO Andy Grove Dies at 79," *Wall Street Journal*, March 22, 2016. When I met with my boss at Intel, it wasn't for him to inspect my work, but rather to figure out how he could help me achieve my key results.

183n **According to Gallup:** Annamarie Mann and Ryan Darby, "Should Managers Focus on Performance or Engagement?" *Gallup Business Journal*, August 5, 2014.

184 **"Feedback is an opinion":** Sheryl Sandberg, *Lean In: Women, Work, and the Will to Lead* (New York: Knopf, 2013).

185 **"want to be 'empowered'":** Josh Bersin, "Feedback Is the Killer App: A New Market and Management Model Emerges," *Forbes*, August 26, 2015.

185 **Today, progressive companies:** Josh Bersin, "A New Market Is Born: Employee Engagement, Feedback, and Culture Apps," joshbersin.com, September 19, 2015.

186 **"As soft as it seems":** "Becoming Irresistible: A New Model for Employee Engagement," *Deloitte Review*, issue 16.

Chapter 18: Culture

215 **these five questions:** https://rework.withgoogle.com/blog/five-keys-to-a-successful-google-team.

216 **High-motivation cultures, they concluded:** Teresa Amabile and Steven Kramer, "The Power of Small Wins," *Harvard Business Review*, May 2011.

220 **His team at LRN:** The study was conducted by the Boston Research Group, the Center for Effective Organizations at the University of Southern California, and Research Data Technology, Inc.

Dedication

248 **As Ken Auletta wrote:** Ken Auletta, "Postscript: Bill Campbell, 1940–2016," *The New Yorker*, April 19, 2016.

251 **"Bill Campbell has been":** Eric Schmidt and Jonathan Rosenberg, *How Google Works* (New York: Grand Central Publishing, 2014).

252 **He "kept Steve Jobs going":** Miguel Helft, "Bill Campbell, 'Coach' to Silicon Valley Luminaries Like Jobs, Page, Has Died," *Forbes*, April 18, 2016.

254 **"always wanted to be":** Podcast with Randy Komisar, soundcloud.com, February 2, 2016.

INDEX

Italic page references indicate figures.

Index

Index

Index

Index

Index

Index